HOW WRITERS
WRITE

HOW WRITERS
WRITE

PAMELA LLOYD

Heinemann
Portsmouth, NH

HEINEMANN EDUCATIONAL BOOKS, INC.
70 Court Street Portsmouth, NH 03801
Offices and agents throughout the world

First published in the United States in 1990 by Heinemann
First published in 1987 in Australia
Thomas Nelson Australia
102 Dodds Street
South Melbourne 3205

ISBN 0 435 08512 3

Designed by Sarn Potter
Cover illustration by Kay Stewart
Typeset in Stymie by Midland Typesetters
Printed in Australia by Southwood Press

CONTENTS

INTRODUCTION

The writers whose conversations are recorded in this book live in Australia, in England, and in the United States, and their work ranges from picture books and poems, to adventure stories, historical and fantasy novels and non-fiction books. They were interviewed in their homes, in hotel rooms and, in the case of one author-illustrator, perched on some spare chairs under the coatracks of a famous exhibition centre! In their own words, the writers describe how their backgrounds and experiences have shaped the way they write and what they write about. The result is some very special insights into how writers live and work.

This book is intended to be used in various ways. You can read it from cover to cover, or you can dip into it, according to your interests or needs. You might want to explore an area of particular interest, such as writing a first draft or simply getting started. Or you might want to improve your knowledge and enjoyment of the work of particular well-known and well-loved writers. The authors' comments on how they tried to write a particular book or poem might lead you to read the completed work—then you would be able to judge for yourself whether they were successful in what they set out to do.

In reading this book you'll discover that there are many different and individual ways to go about this business of writing. There's certainly no single 'correct' way of approaching it—but there's a great deal of pleasure and satisfaction to be obtained from trying.

Pamela Lloyd, 1987

THE WRITERS

For the purposes of this book, the writers have been grouped in the following categories which represent the style of writing for which they are best known. However, I should like to stress that, like many writers, each of them has written books that explore other and different themes.

PICTURE BOOKS
Michael Foreman
Steven Kellogg
Arnold Lobel

HUMOUR
Beverly Cleary
Max Dann
Robin Klein
Sue Townsend
Thomas Rockwell

FANTASY
Lloyd Alexander
Victor Kelleher
Madeleine L'Engle
Jane Yolen

REALISTIC FICTION AND ADVENTURE STORIES
Allan Baillie
Robert Cormier
Michael Dugan
Simon French
Lee Harding
Robert Leeson
Cynthia Voight

HISTORICAL FICTION
Rosemary Sutcliff

POETRY
Eve Merriam
Jack Prelutsky

NON-FICTION
Seymour Simon

'Listening to stories when you are really young
and then reading them as you get older are
really the best ways to becoming a writer.'

Jane Yolen

'I read as much as I can. I read books, not
to pinch ideas, but to see how other authors
write. I read to see how stories are put
together, and to see which sort of story appeals
to me, and to others—and why.'

Simon French

HOW AND WHERE WRITERS WRITE

Every writer works in a different way. They all have their own methods of organising their ideas and of creating the working environment that suits them best—whether it's at the kitchen table, on an express train, or at a farmhouse window overlooking quiet, rolling farmland. Similarly they all have favourite ways of getting the words on paper. Some write longhand, some type, and some use word processors.

Writers Who Are Illustrators, Too

MICHAEL FOREMAN
Land of Dreams, Trick a Tracker and *Panda and the Bunyips* are just three of Michael Foreman's many funny and fantastic illustrated books. His addiction to travel provides endless subject material, and delayed flights or interrupted journeys are ripe with possibilities. When his brain goes numb and blank with the waiting, all sorts of ideas will pop into it—and out comes his sketchbook!

1

'I live and work in both London and Cornwall. When I'm in Cornwall I live in a very busy little seaside town, and my room looks over the harbour. In London I work in an ordinary room where I can look out to the garden. I work every day, and I stay in that room for as long as I can stand it. I'm often working on several things at once — books that I've written, or illustrations that I'm doing for someone else's book — and if I get stuck with one I can always switch to another. If they all grind to a halt, I go for a walk with my sketchbook and pretend I am working!

'It takes me about three or four months to complete one of my own books, from my first idea — to sending it off to the publisher.'

STEVEN KELLOGG

Steven Kellogg is a prolific illustrator, both of his own and of other writers' books. *Can I Keep Him?, Much Bigger than Martin, Ralph's Secret Weapon* **and, of course, his stories about his dog Pinkerton are all well known and well loved. A smiling, comfortable-looking man, Steven Kellogg lives in a very old wooden house in Connecticut in the United States. With him live his family, his two elderly cats, and Pinkerton's successor, a young and very large Great Dane called Angel Annie.**

'I have my own special place where I work. Upstairs in my house there are two little rooms where I do my drawings and my stories. If I get an idea while walking in the woods around my house, I go up there and start writing about it. The dog isn't allowed up there, the cats are not allowed up there — so there are no distractions.

It's very quiet. It overlooks the waterfall and it's a very peaceful place to work.

'I just try to let my mind drift and then, as the story starts to suggest a direction, I write and draw in response to that. I work for a few hours in the morning, usually almost all afternoon, and then sometimes, if a story is really going strongly and the illustrations are going very strongly, I work way into the night until very late.

'The special thing about the picture book is that it's a combination of both words and pictures, and the two of them work together to tell the story. I write with the illustration and with the words as well, and try to make the two of them dance together to tell the story. So they're both equally important to me when I'm putting one of my books together.'

ARNOLD LOBEL
Arnold Lobel lives and works in New York City, in an elegant apartment block on Washington Square. In addition to illustrating other writers' stories, he is the creator of such picture books and stories as *Frog and Toad Are Friends, Fables, The Book of Pigericks, Ming Lo Moves the Mountain*, and *Mouse Tales*.

'I find writing very hard, and I sometimes don't like to write very much because I have no method. I can sit in my chair with my pencil and look at a blank piece of paper every day for six months, and nothing will happen. At another time, I will sit down and in twenty days write an entire book.

'I'm a lazy writer and I write very periodically. I write when I think it's time for me to write another book. I don't write every day.

'Most of my books take me about three months to write. Usually, I write the story first. I don't do the illustrations simultaneously. I don't even try to think visually when I write, because I know I can draw pictures and I never think that I won't be able to do them. But I never know whether I am going to be able to write. When I sit down to write, there is always that question: "Am I going to be able to?"

'I do have a method for drawing. I know for sure that when I sit down for two hours, there's going to be a picture there.

'When I do the illustrations, I sit at my light desk with a piece of tracing paper, and I work entirely out of my imagination. The text tells me what sort of drawing style to use. I can't illustrate a book of romantic poems in the same way that I might do the drawings for a very funny book about the circus.

'I always use a particular kind of drawing paper that I'm comfortable with. I recently bought ten sheets of it, and when I sat down at my desk with it, I couldn't draw! The pencil didn't feel right. The paper turned out to be just slightly different to what I'd asked for. I'd been given the wrong paper and I couldn't draw.'

Writing Humorous Books

'I don't think that a writer can sit down and "try" to write a funny book. I don't try to write funny books, but I think that I have a very wry sense of humour, and without meaning to, I unconsciously see the funny side of everything. I'm afraid it doesn't make me a very dignified person!'

Robin Klein

THOMAS ROCKWELL

Thomas Rockwell is a tall, thin and humourous man who lives with his family in New York State, in a very old house which was once a chicken barn. He writes with a large friendly dog called Charles Bear and a cat called Tin-Tin for company, and outside, a very elderly donkey called Jenny. Best-known for his book *How To Eat Fried Worms*, his other books include *Oatmeal Is Not for Mustaches* and *Hey, Lover Boy*, as well as short stories for adults.

'I used to work on a portable typewriter, because I could never stand the buzz of an electric one. Now I use a word processor, but I'm a little nervous of it. I can see everything on the screen and I feel like I've got this machine on and I'm wasting electricity unless I write quickly. So sometimes I go back to my old typewriter.

'I work every day, writing in the morning and the early afternoon. I like to work where I'm not interrupted, because I lose my concentration and train of thought. I work in a little sort of old junk room upstairs and over the back of the house. I get distracted if I work anywhere else.

'When I'm writing, I don't read what I did the day before. I usually just pick it up each morning and go on from where I finished the day before. I find that better, because otherwise I'd keep revising what I did the day before and then I'd never get ahead.

'I mostly try to finish one piece of writing at a time. Sometimes, if I get stuck, I'll go on to something else, but not often.'

SUE TOWNSEND

Unlike Thomas Rockwell, Sue Townsend doesn't mind distractions around her when she writes. Her family carried on with their lives around her while she wrote *The Secret Diary of Adrian Mole Aged 13¾* and *The Growing Pains of Adrian Mole*. She is also a playwright and her collection *Bazaar & Rummage, Groping for Words, Womberang: Three Plays* has been published.

'I prefer to write where I can hear people moving around somewhere. I quite like writing on trains. I'm not very good at writing in a completely empty house or hotel. I've got my own room for writing in now, and it's been done up and is all very smart, but I still find myself writing at the table in the kitchen. I move around when I write.

'I sometimes write in massive spurts. This is how I wrote *Adrian Mole*. I wrote it in four huge lumps, often over a whole weekend of writing. I do nothing but write and it's a wonderful sort of frenzy to get into. My family will slide coffee and sandwiches under the door, and I'll immerse myself in it. It's very enjoyable. I love it. I laugh and feel very excited and I'm constantly surprised about where the characters and I are going together.

'I write on big pads of paper and I always use a certain sort of fine-line pen. I know it sounds ridiculous, but I couldn't write without one of these pens. I hate typing. It's an ordeal and a drag, and I hate it so much it stops me writing. So I write in very clear, large block letters, so that it's easy to read. Then I get someone else to type it up.'

BEVERLY CLEARY

Beverly Cleary writes from her home in Carmel, California, where her small house overlooks rolling parklands. Although she works on only one book at a time, she sometimes starts it in the middle, or at the end, and then works backwards. Ramona is probably her best-known character, but Beezus, Henry Huggins and Ellen Tebbits are also favourites. Beverly Cleary's novel *Fifteen* is well-known to older readers, while *Mitch and Amy*, *The Mouse and the Motorcycle*, and *Dear Mr Henshaw* are among her other widely read stories.

'I used to start all my books on the second of January. I'd keep writing and usually the book would be finished in June or July. I'd send it off and be on vacation until next second of January. Now, I have so many letters to answer, and other things to do which are connected with being a writer, that it's harder to find the time to write.

'I don't write every day, but when I'm working on a book, I begin writing after breakfast and work until lunchtime. Then I feel that I've done enough for the day. I usually have three books lined up in the back of my mind and all in various stages of "simmering", waiting to come to the boil. But I write one book at a time.

'I write in longhand. I used to write in pencil, but I've discovered an excellent ballpoint pen which I like to use. I write on yellow pads called legal pads, and then I type it up in my very bad typing, revising as I go so that I can see what it looks like. Then I do further revision.

'I'm a very disorganised writer. I rarely begin with chapter one. Sometimes I've written the last chapter first, and then worked back. That's how *Ramona and Her Father* was written. I'd written what now is the ending of the book as a short Christmas story for a magazine, but while I was writing it I was wondering how that family got into that particular situation. I began to work on it and so, really, I wrote the book backwards.'

MAX DANN

A cold cup of tea can distract Max Dann from beginning his day's writing, but not for long, as his popular novels prove. The author of *Adventures with My Worst Best Friend, Going Bananas*, and *Ernest Pickle's Remarkable Robot*, he has also created two remarkable heroines in his stories *Bernice Knows Best* and *One Night at Lottie's House*.

'I do have to discipline myself to write. I usually write from 9.00 am to 5.00 pm. I might take off half an hour for lunch, but otherwise I write straight through all day. I find I have to write at least six hours each day. Inspiration might come only once a week for half an hour, and I can't afford to wait for that. If I go away for a few days and stop writing, I have to build up to that discipline again.

'I have a big old desk that I like to sit at, and I find that little things will throw me off from starting writing. I always like to sit down with a cup of tea to start, but if for some reason my tea has gone cold, that really throws me off. Everything has to be perfect, just to get started. If I'm interrupted, I *can* get back to the writing, but it takes me a while—I have to make another cup of tea! I'm so busy looking for distractions that when one comes along, I'll use it. I don't find it easy to discipline myself.

'I love and hate writing at the same time. Most of the time I hate it, but it gives me more satisfaction when I do it right, than anything else.'

Fantasy Writers

VICTOR KELLEHER
Born in London, Victor Kelleher spent the first twenty years of his life in Africa. These days he lives and works in the New England area of New South Wales. An energetic and enthusiastic man, his books for young people include *The Forbidden Paths of Thual*, *The Hunting of Shadroth*, *Master of the Grove* and *Taronga*.

'I'm very lazy, like anyone else, but the real problem is making myself sit down and work, because I know it's not going to be completely pleasant. The level of concentration is intense. Yet, oddly enough, I like writing because I always think it's too hard for me; and at the same time, that's what I dread about it. I can sit down at 8.00 am to write and be still fiddling around at half past ten. But because I have a full-time job, I can also be very disciplined. I can grab a half hour and cram some work into it.

'Mostly, however, once I start to write, I'm a bit like a terrier. Once I've got those first few pages working, I just don't leave it alone. I keep at it, and do something every day. Even if I'm not writing, I'm planning what I'm going to write and trying out sentences in my mind. I live with it for months and months. And I'm not easy to live with—I'm only half a human being and not all there. That lasts as long as I'm writing the first draft.

'I can work anywhere, but I do tend to get lonely when I'm working a lot. So, much to the consternation of my family, I often like to work in the dining room. I can put up with a certain amount of noise around me, as long as it's not rhythmic noise, because that messes up the rhythms in my head.'

JANE YOLEN
Author of the *Commander Toad* series, Jane Yolen's other books include the beautifully illustrated *An Invitation to the Butterfly Ball* and *Dragon's Blood*, *The Girl Who Cried Flowers and Other Tales*, and *Sleeping Ugly*. She lives with her family in a large white house on the edge of a small section of farmland in Massachusetts. Steep narrow stairs lead to an enormous attic, under a roof which pitches and slides away in all directions. This is where she has set up her desk and her books.

'If you're going to be a professional writer, you have to remember that nobody sets your work times for you; you have to set your own times. I write every morning, even when I don't feel like it. If I stop writing one day, it's going to be harder the next. It's like exercising muscles. If you go for a week without exercising, it's going to ache like crazy when you do. And if you go for a month without exercising, you're going to have lost muscle tone. It's the same thing with writing.

'I work straight on to a typewriter. I never learned to type properly, so I only use four fingers, but I am very fast. I'm so fast that I sometimes feel as if the ideas don't sit in my head, but short-circuit and go right out through my fingers, because there are times when stories come out that I wasn't really expecting. That's such fun, and it's what I love about writing.

'I sit there and type until nothing else comes out. That could be for two minutes, or it could be for seven hours. When nothing more comes, I stop and I put it aside. I may then decide that I have something else I'm interested in writing, and I reach into my ideas file and pull out something else I feel like doing, because I work on any number of things at the same time.

'I'm a very organised person. Pretend you are sitting at my desk. On the left are two double-drawer filing cabinets. In the bottom of those cabinets are files full of essays or speeches that I'm writing. On top of them are the books that I've sold. They may still be in various stages. I may have sold the novel, but only have sold it by writing an outline and a couple of chapters. There may be all the revisions I've done of each novel. There may be ten different versions of a picture book that I've done.

'On the other side of my desk, in alphabetical order, are all my starts of things that I haven't yet finished. Again, in each folder will be all the versions of the story. Some of the folders might only hold a paragraph, or maybe a page. Some of them hold chapter of a book that I've just started, or notes, but each of those are things which I'm really working on.

'Underneath that is a file drawer of stuff that I've more or less decided doesn't work. Again, it's in alphabetical order by the titles. I haven't exactly put them away, because I may go back to them.

'I always had a special place to write in, right in the middle of the house, but I wouldn't try to write until everyone had gone out for a while. Sometimes I may wake up in the middle of the night, or get up early in the morning, and sit and write for an hour or so, still in my nightgown.

'When my children became too noisy I built an office up in the attic, which is enormous, and that's where I now write. I have one whole side wall filled with my folklore books, and the other wall filled with my children's books and my encyclopaedias, plus, of course, my big desk and my filing cabinets.'

LLOYD ALEXANDER
This author of such fantasy novels as *The Black Cauldron*, *The Book of Three*, and *Westmark* lives in a small house in Pennsylvania. His funny and wistful caricatures and sketches decorate the walls of his study, where he reads, writes and makes music.

'I get up at four o'clock in the morning and go into my workroom. There I'll write for as long as I feel like it, and it's always difficult. Usually that will be for about three hours, and if I'm lucky, I'll get half a page complete. That's a good morning's work. But while some days are good, some days are bad.

'I don't write in longhand because I'm left-handed and I keep covering over what I've written if I write by hand. I use a typewriter because I can see what I do. I don't want to use a word processor because I need to feel the connection that comes with actually typing out those words.

'My workroom is nothing fancy. There's a table and a chair and a couch, and that's about all.

'When I write, I've discovered that, if the writing is going well, then that's the time to stop for the day. If the work is going badly, then I must stay with it until I've fought through that particular problem. This is important, because when I stop and the work is going well, I can come back the next day on the crest of my energy. I come back to a high point which I can get into immediately, and the work goes better. If I stop when I have a problem, and come back to it the next day, then I come back to a problem and it pulls me down.'

MADELEINE L'ENGLE

Madeleine L'Engle and her family divide their time between two homes, one in New York City and the other amongst the hills and woods of Connecticut.

When in Connecticut she writes at a desk in her study under the attic roof. There is a piano near her desk, so that she can swing around in her chair and reach the keyboard when she feels like a break from writing. It was this house which provided the setting for her novel *A Wrinkle in Time*, the first of her Time trilogy. Her base in New York City, in the library of the magnificent John of God Cathedral, provided the setting for another of her novels, *The Young Unicorns*.

'I can write anywhere. When I was twelve I was put into an English boarding school where I shared a room with five other girls. We weren't allowed to be alone for a second, so I learnt to make my own privacy in the middle of all the sound and fury. I put an imaginary force field of silence around me, which became a very good discipline. It means that I don't have to have special places to write in. I write in hotels or aeroplanes—anywhere I can have a piece of paper and a pen.

'The room where I mostly write is in my house which sits on the ridge of a mountain in Connecticut in the United States. This house has withstood over 200 years of storms, and it used to be an old summer boarding house. My writing room was full of chickens in 1946, so when we arrived here I knocked out some walls and cleaned it up. My children called it "Mother's Ivory Tower", even though it's a type of attic rather than a tower. This is the house that the Murrays lived in, in my book *A Wrinkle in Time*.'

Writing Realistic Fiction and Adventure Stories

ALLAN BAILLIE
Author of *Adrift, Little Brother*, and *Riverman*, Allan Baillie works from his home which is perched on a steep hill high above Pittwater, a beautiful stretch of water north of Sydney. Even so, his study looks out over the back garden, with not one of his beloved boats in sight!

'The writing starts off from the moment I start thinking about the ideas. I find that if I fiddle around before I start, too many wasted ideas get tossed around. So I just start writing, forcing and pushing the thoughts out, because I know that I'm going to take two, three or four drafts to write the book. It doesn't matter how bad the writing is. What matters is that it's all down. I write on a computer, which means that everything I want is there. If it's a bad idea, or badly written, I just press a button and it's gone.

'When I used to work as a journalist, I only had four days in the week to write. I try to write from 9.00 am to 5.00 pm, but sometimes I'm tempted—and I go sailing. Otherwise, I go into my little office and stay there until I feel I'm miserable enough to go out.

'During the awful first draft, I have to make myself go in and finish a chapter, or whatever I've set myself to complete, before I allow myself to stop. However, near to the end of the first draft, or when the characters have really taken off, then I'll work seven hours straight and not stop for dinner or something like that.

'I write straight through, in the order of the story. I don't use an outline because by then it's very strongly in my mind.'

SIMON FRENCH
Simon French wrote and had his first book, *Hey, Phantom Singlet*, published while still at high school. Since then he's written *Cannily Cannily* and *All We Know*. He lives in a small white-painted farmhouse outside Sydney.

'I have half-a-dozen settings around the house where I like to work, depending on the weather and what my mood is. I usually need a pot of tea and a view! Most of the tables where I work are beside windows, or outdoors. Mostly I need peace and quiet.

'My writing tends to weave in and out of my other daily activities because I don't write all the time. It fits in with my job and it fits in according to how much energy I have. I'm not particularly methodical with time allocations for my writing. However, when I wrote *All We Know*, I did sit down every day and work on it for a couple of hours first thing in the morning. And I spent the middle part of the day thinking about it and about what story angle I could tackle next, or how I could add further insight and depth to the characters I was writing about. I concluded most days with either typing up, or perhaps some jigsawing together of chapter elements.

'My ideas often come "on the run"—when I'm stuck in a traffic jam, flat out at work, or at home reading the paper. I think about whatever story I'm working on much of the time, and from this the sparks for new ideas sometimes happen. I used to jot down thoughts and approaches in a note pad I kept in the car. These days I tend to refine my thoughts in my mind before I write out actual text, but I try and keep a notepad with me just in case.'

'I don't write stories in any particular order. I don't start at the beginning and work methodically through to the end. With *Cannily Cannily* the first things I wrote were the opening and final chapters. Everything else was written completely out of order, as I thought of each segment of the story. While I was fired up over a particular idea or conversation that I wanted to happen I'd write it out and, later on, look at where in the storyline it needed to be slotted in.

'I really have to concentrate to write. If I've an idea that's mapped out and ready to be written down, I have to do it straight away. Sometimes it seems I've lost so many good ideas—the words were fantastic, the phrasing just right, but because I was interrupted or didn't write them down when I should have, I've lost them forever. Sometimes I can stay on the wavelength of an idea for only two or three lines, so I have to rule a line under that and try another approach. When I was writing *All We Know*, I might have had four or five different parts of the story, totally unrelated, written out on the same sheet of paper. I also managed to write out two whole chapters in one go, which for me was really something. It was one of the key moments of the whole story, and it came out in a great rush. I had a sore hand after that effort!

'I write in longhand, scribbled out in pencil or pen on the back of scrap or computer paper, sometimes notepads. I don't like writing on lined paper. It has to be blank.

'Once I've something substantial written, I then go

back and cut it up, sticky tape the bits together in some sort of order, and type it out.'

ROBERT CORMIER

Robert Cormier is quietly spoken and reserved—in unexpected contrast to his fast-paced, exciting and unsettling stories, such as *The Chocolate War* **and** *Beyond the Chocolate War, I Am the Cheese, After the First Death,* **and** *The Bumblebee Flies Anyway.* **He writes in his small study in his house in Massachusetts.**

'I'm a journalist so I write every day, but when I'm at home I get to my typewriter reasonably early in the morning after reading the paper and having breakfast. I work in a little study, where I can see into the dining room and know what's going on.

'However, I don't sit there for six or seven agonising hours. I don't start writing and think that I have to write four pages or ten pages today. I write with the sense of wondering what's going to happen to my character today.

'I may get up and walk around. I type for a while and then get up and look out of the window, and then go back to the typewriter. I write in fits and starts, but I do it constantly.

'I write chronologically, in scenes. I can't seem to go on with the next scene until the one I'm working on is finished. I know in my mind where I want to get to, but sometimes this turns out differently from what I was expecting. This happens because I let the characters move.'

CYNTHIA VOIGT

The American writer, Cynthia Voigt, lives with her family in a large old wooden house in the historic naval town of Annapolis, on Maryland's beautiful Chesapeake Bay. She writes about her love of the Bay in her novels *Homecoming* and *Dicey's Song*. She is also the author of *A Solitary Blue,* and the fantasy *The Callender Papers.*

'I write upstairs in a little spare room which has a desk and a very large comfortable chair. I try to work my day so that it's blocked out in sections. I have a four-hour block in the morning when nobody is at home, and that's when I write. In the afternoon I teach, and after dinner I'm supposed to do the preparation and corrections for the next afternoon's class.

'However, when I'm really working on something, I wait until the family goes out the door, turn on the typewriter, feed a sheet of paper in, read where I was yesterday and continue. Then I can write quite happily for four, five or six hours. I rush out to my class in the afternoon, with no preparation done, and come back and go on writing.

'I don't mind leaving the writing each afternoon to go to work, because when it isn't really coming right you can't force it. You have to leave it alone for a while, and going away to do something else helps me do this.

'When I'm not wallowing in it, I'll write for an hour or an hour and a half, every morning.'

ROBERT LEESON
Moving from room to room
in his small suburban
London house, Robert
Leeson chases the sun as he
writes each day. His novels,
reflecting science fiction
and fantasy elements, include *The Third Class Genie,*
The Demon Bike Rider, and *Challenge in the Dark,* and
for young adult readers, *It's My Life.* Best-known for
the Grange Hill School novels, he also writes adult
novels and historical fiction.

'There's a small half-room in my house where I moved
all my writing stuff after my children moved into their
own places. That's where I type. But mostly I move from
room to room in the house, following the sunshine.

'When I've got down to actually writing the book, I
like to have sheets of rough paper stuck on a clipboard,
so that I can carry it around and sit and write or, better
still, I can put it down and sit and stare out of the
window.

'When the ideas and the words start flowing, I pick
up my pen and write on to the clipboard. But when I'm
really in the last stages of a book, then I like to get into
the room, shut the door, get on the typewriter and work
steadily morning and afternoon until I've finished it.'

MICHAEL DUGAN
Michael Dugan's writing
interests range far and
wide. Well known as the
author of the *Australian
Fact Finders* and *Famous
Australians* series, he has
also written picture books like *A House for Wombats,*

humorous stories such as *Great Overland Riverboat Race*, and the novels *Dingo Boy* and *Melissa's Ghost.*

'I write at a table under a window that looks out on to a cherry-plum tree. My most used reference books are on a shelf next to the table, and while I'm writing I like to have the table clear of everything but the book and my notes for it.

'My first draft is written in longhand. Then I go through it and make changes with a different coloured ink, before I start the first typed draft.

'The time it takes to write a book varies. *Dingo Boy* took ten years for the ideas to come together, but I wrote it in fourteen days. *Melissa's Ghost* was written over four months and then put aside for nearly eighteen months. The longest I've spent is the fifteen months it took to write *There Goes the Neighbourhood*, though this isn't a children's book.'

LEE HARDING

Unlike many writers, Lee Harding has deliberately positioned his desk to face a wall and not a view—he finds that this helps his concentration. His novels include *Children of Atlantis*, *Return to Tomorrow*, *Displaced Person*, and *Waiting for the End of the World.*

'I have to work every day—it's self-discipline, the hardest discipline of all. I work a certain number of hours each day. Some days I don't, because sometimes it's important to break routine and recharge the batteries. I've never experienced "writer's block", because if I find that I can't move a story in a particular direction, I put that story aside and work on something else, and come back to it later. So it's common for me to be working on several things at once. I can begin the next book, while I'm halfway through the one I'm working on, and then can put that aside to give me something to start with when I've finished the current book.

'But I need to go to the desk and sit down and get on with it! Inspiration is a rare thing, and unless I am working at my desk each day, there'd be little chance for that moment of inspiration (which is a clear view of my objective) to occur. Writing is mostly slogging hard work, and you have to discipline yourself to do that.

'I'm very fussy and fastidious about where I work. I think because my imaginative life is so chaotic, and the juggling act involved in keeping all the facets of a book working is so consuming, that I like to have my study as orderly as possible. I need a quiet secluded place to write, without distractions. I make sure I'm not facing a window, or have a window beside me, so that I can focus on what I'm doing. I write facing a wall, which is a trick that works for me.

'I've never written in longhand. I had my first typewriter when I was eleven. I've recently moved over to working on a word processor, which lets me rub out and rework as I go along. I don't have to rip the whole page out of the typewriter and start again.'

Writing Historical Fiction

ROSEMARY SUTCLIFF
Rosemary Sutcliff lives and works in a very old stone cottage in the beautiful village of Arundel in Sussex, England. Her small and crowded study looks

over green lawns and ancient trees, and her dogs share the spare chair while she works. Her deep interest in the ancient and Roman history of Britain have inspired novels such as *The Lantern Bearers* and *Warrior Scarlet*, while books such as *The Truce of the Games* arose out of her awareness of other ancient worlds.

'I don't set myself a certain time to write every day, because I get too many interruptions when I write at home. I don't try to start writing until late in the morning, and then I work until bedtime. I work whenever there's the opportunity, so that I can feel free to drop it and go and do other things. I don't have any difficulty in putting the writing down and picking it up later, as long as it isn't in the middle of a very tense passage, because I know it's a draft and I'll be rewriting it again.

'I write in longhand, in large (preferably red) exercise books. I feel better with a red exercise book than any other colour. After I have finished all my drafts and polished the manuscript, then I send it away to be typed.

'The only audience I write for is me. Somebody once said that what makes a good children's writer is a sort of unlived pocket of childhood in the writer. I think that I write mainly for this unlived pocket of childhood in myself. I don't write for other children.'

Writers Who Are Poets

JACK PRELUTSKY
Creator of poetry collections such as *The New Kid on the Block*, *Nightmares: Poems to Trouble Your Sleep*, and *Rolling Harvey down the*

Hill, Jack Prelutsky writes in a large, book-filled study in his home in New Mexico. He will often pick up a guitar and sing his poems to made-up tunes, to see how they sound.

'I save all my ideas notebooks — I have at least fifty — and when I'm ready to write another book of poems I start working my way through all the notebooks. Normally I don't feel like I have to write all the time, but when I start a book of poems I work for about seven weeks of intense writing, working non-stop for sixteen or twenty-two hours a day. I live in my bathrobe and start to stink a little bit, and sleep in my study, and just get up and start writing again. I can't turn it off. I'm supercharged.

'In my notebooks, the ideas could be in the form of a single nonsense word that I've made up, or a few lines of rhyme that may be the beginning of a poem, or the end of one.

'I have three work stations in my study. One is my big recliner chair, one is my desk, and the other is my word processor. And I tend to work in a circle between them all. The word processor is an easy form of storage of ideas. I can have a lot of fun crosscutting and pasting up very quickly. I can change words here and there, and it's quick. It gives me the option of trying things which would be cumbersome otherwise, because a lot of poetry writing is about finding the right word or the right rhythm — it's about trying something out, seeing that it doesn't work and trying something else.

'The word processor helps me to visualise things more quickly. I can write a poem in four different ways in thirty seconds. I can take verses and switch them around — maybe the second half of the third verse should really be the first half of the fifth verse.

'Then, when I see what I've written up on the screen, I sit in my chair and I work with a guitar and sing it, improvising or making up the melody. That helps me hear what it sounds like.

'I've started to write poems in the bath. It's very relaxing and warm, and I lie back and do a lot of good thinking in the bath. I shrivel a bit and go all wrinkled, because I keep old magazines to read there. One day I was reading an article on wolves, and all the "S"s and the wolves and the water and the washing started coming together in my head. Some friends had given me a pen and a pad of paper on which you can write under water, because they knew that I liked to write in the bath, and I started a poem called "The Wolf is at the Laundromat".

'The ending came from the article on wolves which had put a pun into my mind. That lead to the beginning, so I had to make up a little story to get from the beginning to the end. I had a lot of fun with sound combinations and words:

"A wolf is at the Laundromat,
it's not a wary stare-wolf.
it's short and fat, it tips hat,
unlike the scary glare-wolf.
It combs its hair, it clips its toes,
it is a fairly rare wolf,
that's only there to clean its clothes—
it is a wash-and-wear-wolf."'

EVE MERRIAM
Eve Merriam lives and works high up in an apartment block in New York City, where the noise of traffic, sirens and people are a constant backdrop to her days. Her poems are a reflection of the world around her, and her collections include *No Rhyme For*

Silver, Fresh Paint: New Poems, and *A Sky Full of Poems.*

'I often get ideas when I'm walking. I used to be caught too often without a pencil and paper, and then I'd be anxious until I could get home and write it down. Now I keep a stub of pencil and a notebook in my pocket, and I try to write something down even if it is just the one word. I don't like to sit at a desk and I do like to walk, but I never go out and deliberately walk to try to get an idea—it's always a surprise. But I find that somehow the physical excercise releases something in my head.

'The process of writing the poem from that idea may sometimes take a long while. There were many weeks of seeing a derelict car outside my apartment every day before I started to write anything. The image had to permeate my brain. Then I worked on the poem "Landscape" over many months. I don't, however, consistently work at a poem every day. I'd go batty. I work for a couple of hours until I get bleary eyed and I have to stop. Then I'll put it away and, depending on how compulsively I want to finish it, I'll go back to it. I live by myself, so I can work at night if I want to.

'One of the advantages of being a poet is that you don't need a grand piano or a sculptor's studio to work. You can carry a word around in your pocket, so you don't need to have much equipment. Often when I'm writing a poem, there's only one word in it which needs refining, and I can carry that word around in my pocket and keep refining it over months. It's like a jigsaw puzzle, or a crossword puzzle where I need just one word with the right number of syllables to fit the rhythm of the line. Eventually I'll get the word I want.

'Occasionally I've invented words—where for a particular purpose I need harsh sounds, for example. But mostly I don't make up words.'

Writing Non-Fiction

SEYMOUR SIMON
A lifetime's fascination with science combined with natural curiosity and a wish to share the excitement of his observations have led Seymour Simon to write an enormously diverse range of books. They range from investigating space to making paper aeroplanes, and include Body Sense—Body Nonsense, Ghosts, The Smallest Dinosaur, **and** Hidden Worlds: Pictures of the Invisible. **He lives in New York, on Long Island.**

'I write in a very quiet place in my home, when I need to be away from too much activity. However, when I'm concentrating enormously on writing, it doesn't really make any difference what else is going on around me. And I do find writing a very lonely activity, so when the telephone rings during the time that I'm writing, I'm overjoyed.

'My writing is the way I make my living, so I try to keep to a writer's schedule. I sit down to write first thing in the morning, right after breakfast, and I try not to let anything distract me from that. I find that the most difficult thing is to get myself started. Once I've begun and I've got a sentence down, then there's no problem.

'I'll continue writing for as long as I can, which is often into the early afternoon. Then after lunch I do all the things that go with my writing. I send letters off to get information that I might want. I talk to my editors and answer letters from children or librarians.

'I try not to put off writing each day, because the longer I put it off the more difficult it is to get back into the project I'm working on. If I've been working on a project for a long time, and I've dropped it for a while,

I come back with the feeling that I've already done that and it's not as interesting as before.

'I used to write using a typewriter. By the time I finished a page there'd be so many erasures and so many pencil scribblings that I'd retype it, changing more as I worked. In the end whether I changed things depended on my energy level, because it took so much energy to keep retyping the page.

'I've been using a word processor for the last two years, and this makes it all much easier. I edit and rewrite each word as I go. I just keep changing it and changing it.

'How long it takes to write a book depends a lot on its length and who it's for. A book for kindergarten to third grade will take me a shorter time to write, but a much longer time to rewrite, because every word is thought about and changed again and again. I might rewrite that book six times. It's much easier to write for older children than for younger children, because I don't have to explain everything.

'But writing a book is a lot more than siting down and getting the words on to paper. It's thinking about the book and incubating the idea which takes a long time.'

WHERE DO IDEAS COME FROM?

Writers and illustrators draw their ideas from all sorts of sources: from dreams, childhood memories, newspaper articles, from conversations with their children or friends—the spark for a story can come from almost anywhere!

Picture Books

MICHAEL FOREMAN

As a boy, Michael Foreman delivered newspapers. On his route he met one of the teachers at the local art school, who asked him to dig some clay for the modelling class he ran. This job led to the suggestion that Michael attend art classes himself. For Michael, not very good at anything at school except football, this was the chance that set him on his way to becoming an artist and a writer.

'Ideas usually come from two sources. I do a lot of travelling, and while I'm in a foreign country I do lots of drawing in sketchbooks. Then there might be something which suddenly appears in a newspaper or on television and I'll think: "Ah! I'd like to do a story about that subject." And so I have the germ of an idea, and in amongst my sketchbooks there will probably be the most appropriate setting for that idea to happen.

'Sometimes ideas arise out of something else that I'm doing, so that there can be ten ideas for stories lying around in my mind at any one time. I'm usually working on several books at the one time and they'll be at different stages. One will be nearing completion, one will be in the hard slog stage, another will be just starting out. The story may be a kind of an antidote to the others. I might have wanted to do something very silly as a change alongside the other books I was working on.

'Once I woke up at 3 o'clock in the morning with a silly picture of an elephant on a skateboard in my mind. By breakfast time I'd written the story. It seemed to work, so I then sat down over the next three or four weeks and did the pictures. That became the book *Trick a Tracker*.

'I've just visited my brothers whom I haven't seen for a couple of years, and that reminded me of when my eldest brother came back from the army when I was a very small boy. He'd been in Egypt and he came back with a quilt. It had embroidered pyramids and palm trees and camels on it, and it was on my mother's bed for many years where I saw it every day.

'Now, I've been wanting to do a book about a boy who has a mysterious journey during the night, and I've suddenly realised that this quilt can be the way to make this idea work. The boy could go to bed and the quilt would be over his bed, and during the night he could slowly unravel it in his dreams—have an adventure, obviously in the desert and in the pyramids. By using the thread, he could find his way out of some terrible predicament that he's got himself into, and wake up in the morning safe in his bed. Of course the quilt would be totally threadbare, but in the bottom of the bed, there'd be some sand . . .

'Now this may not work out, but it seems to. Again,

it has a peculiar logic to it. But this is an idea which has been lying around for a while, and it's just a conversation with my brothers which seems to have suddenly provided the missing link.'

STEVEN KELLOGG

When Steven Kellogg was a child, he loved to write stories and illustrate them, particularly with pictures of animals. These were usually made up for his two younger sisters, and he would do them on the spot while they watched. When the story was all together he would sit between them with a pile of paper on his lap, and pass the illustrations to them as he told the story. They called it 'telling stories on paper'.

'I usually have just a small piece of an idea, or a little thought, or a little picture in my mind, and then I put that on the paper and try to let it grow in whatever way it wants to grow, to start to move. If something starts to happen, then I try to follow it and tune into the story. Sometimes I'll get an idea that seems to be an excellent ending, or a character that suggests the story. Often, it's a feeling that I want to share.

'One of the first books I wrote and illustrated, called *Can I Keep Him?*, has a character who's a little bit autobiographical. When I was a little boy I loved animals and had a great desire to have a pet. My parents weren't particularly fond of animals and didn't feel a need to have one in the house. I used to bring home stray animals and I'd even adopt the animals that were owned by my neighbours and had perfectly good homes. I remember that feeling—that yearning for a pet or something that I could love and share my home and life with. And that feeling became the book *Can I Keep Him?*'

ARNOLD LOBEL

Author-illustrator Arnold Lobel once found the ideas for a book because he broke his foot. It was wintertime and, because he had a plaster cast on his foot, the snow on the ground outdoors meant that he could not escape his desk. There was nothing else he could do—he had to write. And the result was his book *Fables.*

'The ideas for my stories are always related to my own life. They come from a collision of all different kinds of things, like a patchwork quilt. The *Frog and Toad* stories began when my daughter had a pet toad, but all the incidents in the books are expressing good and bad feelings that I had about my life.

'The ideas that start a story can be conscious or unconscious. In some of the *Frog and Toad* stories I was very conscious. I knew exactly the incident which created the story. Before setting pencil to paper I had thought: "That would make an interesting story."

'The ideas for the books can be deliberately chosen, or they can come out of how I have been feeling. When I was writing *Fables* I was very confused, and no matter how much I wanted to, I couldn't come to any conclusions about my life. That book turned out to be very ordered, and every story had a moral. It even looked very framed and ordered.'

Humour

ROBIN KLEIN

Robin Klein can't remember a time when she didn't have a pencil in one hand and a sheet of paper in the other. She grew up in a family of nine children, and her storytelling parents encouraged all of them to read and write family newspapers and plays. She discovered by accident, later in her life, that she had a knack for writing for children, and since then has had many books published, including *Junk Castle, Thing, Hating Alison Ashley, Boss of the Pool, People Might Hear You* and, of course, *Penny Pollard's Diary* and *Penny Pollard's Letters*. Here she describes how she came to write about Penny.

'I'd been commissioned to write a story as a serial for the *School Magazine* produced by the Education Department for New South Wales. I used an old short story which I'd written and which hadn't worked originally, and in that story the girl's voice takes the direct form which is the diary. *School Magazine* then decided not to use the story (perhaps because of Penny's grammar!) and one of the editors suggested that it would be a good picture book. One other publisher turned it down, and then it was published with Ann James' wonderful illustrations.

'Because Penny was such a strong character, it was quite easy to write in the diary form. I would just put myself into her mind and pretend that I was Penny writing it. I also had a good structure to work with in the story, because there was a very clear plot. I knew that I wanted to use an old lady in an old people's home.

'That idea came when I was working in a school in Melbourne. I used to take some of the kids out on excursions, and I was horrified at some of the attitudes they had to old people. I wanted to write something where the plot had a kid forming a friendship with a really old person. Without preaching, I wanted to get across the idea that it can be a rewarding relationship, so I knew that the old lady would have to be seen through Penny's eyes.'

SUE TOWNSEND

Adrian Mole is another hero met through the pages of his diary. Author Sue Townsend describes herself as a 'secret' writer for nineteen years before she began to be published, and it was during this time that she created Adrian and the whole Mole family.

'The idea for *The Secret Diary of Adrian Mole Aged 13¾* was sparked off by my eldest son saying to me: "Why can't we be like other families? Why can't we go to safari parks on Sundays?"

'It's the only real line from life that's actually in the book. He said: "Why do you always sit around reading the papers on Sundays?" And that was the first sort of quite kind criticism of the family and the whole family set-up that he ever actually made. He must have been thinking it for years, and it just reminded me that at that age you have to stand back from your parents. You look at them and you're horrified by them. You think they're awful. Their clothes are terrible, and so is the style of furniture they choose, what they read — everything about them. Suddenly you're sort of alienated from them.

'I think that it's part of growing and developing into a person, but it can be very awkward and painful for people. But it did remind me how I felt when I was a teenager. I loathed and detested most things about my family and my relations and so on. And suddenly the whole Mole family came down in one piece, along with Adrian Mole's voice and the tone of his voice.

'I made it a diary because diaries are supposed to be secret, and in this book I wanted the absolutely true feelings of a boy. When I started out, the idea was to write about the sensitive side of a boy.'

BEVERLY CLEARY

Beverly Cleary began writing when she discovered a pile of typing paper in the linen cupboard of the first home she and her husband owned. But when she sat down to write a book about a girl, Henry Huggins made his first appearance!

'I often don't know where the ideas come from. I start with a character or an incident and begin to write, and as I write the character grows. So the story grows, and after much muddling around, it finally takes shape.

'One idea came from my son. When he was in the fourth grade he was absolutely disgusted with school, books, reading and everything else. When I asked him what he wanted to read about, he said: "Motorcycles! I wrote *The Mouse and the Motorcycle* which pleased him so much and he read it twice.'

THOMAS ROCKWELL

When Thomas Rockwell was young, all he wanted to do was play professional basketball. But he wasn't quick enough, and even worse, he didn't grow tall enough. After studying art for two weeks, he started writing short stories instead.

'The idea for *How to Eat Fried Worms* arose when I went to New York City to see an editor about another manuscript. She hadn't liked the manuscript at all. It was 150 typewritten pages, and she picked out one page and thought that was good and suggested I write something less fanciful—maybe more realistic.

'So there I was, driving back home and trying to think of a more realistic book, and I was really feeling terrible that my manuscript had been rejected. I felt as if I had been eating worms, and you know that old jingle "nobody loves me, everybody hates me, think I'm gonna eat worms . . ." I didn't think of that, but it was that sort of feeling. All of a sudden the idea popped into my head: "Why don't I write a book about a boy who eats worms?"

'I liked the idea because it was funny, and a sort of rebellious thing to do—thumbing your nose at the adult world:

"Eat your vegetables!"

"No, I'm going to eat my worms."

'So I'm still driving my car, and the next thing I thought of was the title: *How to Eat Fried Worms*. It really isn't a book on how to eat fried worms, but it's a good title because it's sort of intriguing.

'Then came the difficult part: *why* is somebody going to eat worms? And even before I got home, I thought: "Well, make it a bet."'

MAX DANN
Ideas can come from memories. Max Dann really knew a boy like Peter Dusting, one of the main characters in his book *Adventures with My Worst Best Friend*.

'I used to take notes of people or things that I saw, but I don't do that any more because I found that I didn't use them. However, writing down thoughts and ideas does keep them fresh in my memory.

'I get a lot of my ideas from remembering things from when I was a kid. I grew up in the western suburbs of Melbourne, and I remember the things that happened to me and the kids around me.

'The ideas come from the characters more than anything else. As I spend more time developing the characters and they begin to emerge, they often create much of the plot themselves. Without good solid characters, the best plot in the world is not going to work.'

Fantasy

VICTOR KELLEHER

Like many writers, Victor Kelleher writes novels that embrace many themes and genres. But it is his fantasy novels for which he is best known, and he sometimes finds the ideas for these within his dreams.

'I get ideas from everywhere. An idea will jump out at me right in the middle of a conversation and I'll think: "I can use this". I then usually find an excuse to get away and jot it down somewhere.

'I can be out running in the mornings and I'll get an idea out of nowhere. I have many ready places from which I can get ideas, or at least fragments of ideas. There's more than just one idea in a book. There's a central idea, and then, to get it to work, I need many more ideas coming in sideways at it to make the idea more than just the simple notion it was originally.

'I also get those central ideas, and those sideways "pop" ideas, from dreams. I keep a very careful record of my dreams. I don't mean that I wake up every morning and write down faithfully everything I can remember. But every now and again I wake up in the morning, and sometimes in the middle of the night, and I've had a really "hot" dream. I *know* it's a book dream, and in those cases I write it down immediately, or what I can remember of it. Sometimes it's a fragment of an idea. Sometimes I get very very detailed sequences. Sometimes it's a whole still picture.

'Sometimes my dreams are moving and sometimes they're still, the same way as in movies. The stills, especially, have an enormous amount of detail. I've discovered, like many people, that if soon after you've woken you write down what happened in your dream, the business of recalling it aids recall, and you actually dredge up much more of the dream than you at first realised was there.

'So, for example, a book of mine called *The Makers*, has its basic idea hingeing on a warrior cult. And that came from a dream in which I was an onlooker to a strange group of peculiarly armed people, in a funny situation which I didn't understand. The dream didn't make any sense, so I wrote it down and then added ideas to make sense of it, and in making sense of it I made it into a book.

'The idea of Shadroth, in my book *The Hunting of Shadroth*, is a memory dating from the *most* horrifying nightmare I ever had in my life, when I was about twenty-one years old. I took the figure of Shadroth from that nightmare, although I didn't use it in a nightmarish way.

'I also get ideas from still pictures in my head, which are memories that stay there for some reason. These visuals become the bases for my books in the same way that dreams become the bases—not necessarily because the idea they contain is so good, though that sometimes is true, but because the atmospherics are so very powerful in those half-remembered, half-imagined scenes. As a writer I have to account for and reproduce that atmosphere, and I do that through a selection of detail, through a selection of visual image. So I draw from all these sources and it's very rarely that one idea equals one book. I collect a lot of things and I paste them together.

'I keep a little file called "Ideas", and a more disgusting collection of little fragments of paper you wouldn't hope to meet in all your life. You'd wonder how anyone could get anything out of them at all! They're not beautifully written ideas, well written out. They're bits torn off the edges of newspapers, where I've had an idea and scribbled it down on the unprinted edge with someone's borrowed biro. I never bother to rewrite them, I just stick them in a file.

'Even when I record bits of dream, I do it very untidily. I write these ideas very badly—not only is the handwriting bad, but the idea is often badly expressed. And that's for a purpose. I don't want to spend a lot of time writing ideas down. They're just trigger mechanisms, to trigger off my memory, which is very good. Every now and then I remind myself that they're there, and I browse through the file so that the ideas don't go from my memory completely.'

JANE YOLEN

Jane Yolen began writing when she was in first grade. She used to write poems, and she quickly learnt that writing her reports in rhyme usually won her a gold star. She sang folk songs with her father, and her love of fairytales, storytelling and balladry, colours her stories with fantasy.

'Well, for me there are two places where any story starts, and sometimes it takes a long time for the two places to come together.

'The first place is something outside myself. Maybe I'll read something. Maybe I'll see a photographer or a picture, or hear someone say something. Often a song I hear says something to me. Occasionally I'll hear another story which will start me. But that's all outside me.

'The second place is an inside emotion, and it sometimes takes many years between getting the outside idea and finding the corresponding emotion, before the story idea can become real and become complete.

'For example, my story *The Girl Who Cried Flowers* began because many years ago I saw a picture by Botticelli called "Spring", in which Spring is wandering across a beautiful canvas with flowers coming out of her mouth. I'd just written a story in which something comes out of someone's mouth, so I thought: "Where else could flowers come from?" Out of the nose is gross, from the ears seems a little ridiculous, but "crying" flowers seemed to have a nice feeling to it. I wrote one or two paragraphs about that, but I didn't have a story. I just had an image and it sat that way in my files for about five years.

'Later something sad and difficult happened to a friend of mine, and the feeling it gave me fitted with this picture I had of a girl crying flowers. I already had the two or three paragraphs that just described the girl who cried flowers. That was what I'd set down and put aside for a number of years, and then the answer and the emotion within happened. I was ready to tell the story.'

LLOYD ALEXANDER

Although he began writing for adults, and did this for many years, Lloyd Alexander has written many popular novels for children, including *The Book of Three*. Here, he talks about the way an idea evolved into the story *Time Cat*.

'The ideas come from two places: they come from inside your head, and outside your head. The outside part of it is everything that you see or do, every experience that you have. But it's not as important as the inside part of it. In other words, everything that you see and do in your life somehow goes into your imagination, which works on it and processes it and does things to it that you're not even aware of.

'One of my cats gave me the idea for a book. I'd sit in my workroom, and one of my favourite cats would come into my room, and I'd never actually see him come in. All of a sudden I'd turn around and there he was. I'd greet him and I'd compliment him on how well his tail looked, and pat him and have a nice conversation.

I'd turn back, and he would be gone and I'd never see him get up and leave. This amused me because it would always happen. I began having fun with this, purely for my own amusement. I began to think: "Now, how does he do that? I never see him come in. I never see him leave. He's an enchanted cat."

'I played with the idea, thinking: "Well, he goes somewhere, and the saying is that a cat has nine lives." Well, I thought, he doesn't have to have them one after the other. They can be available to him whenever he wants them. I'm sure he disappears and he's going to one of his various lives.

'This, for a while, was just my own private joke. I made nothing of it. And then, all of a sudden, one day the ideas came to me. Hey now! Wait a minute! There is a structure here! If he can go to his nine different lives, where would he go and could he take somebody with him? I'd like to go with him. Why couldn't he take someone along?

'Here are nine lives. And wait a minute! Here are nine chapters and they could be nine different countries in the past.

'And all of a sudden, there's that peculiar moment when all these things that don't mean anything to you for a long time somehow come together and click in your mind. I immediately wrote on a scrap of paper, one sentence: "A boy and his cat go to nine different countries in the past." But I know I won't forget that idea.'

Realistic Fiction and Adventure Stories

SIMON FRENCH

'The ideas don't all happen at once, they happen over a period of time. What I invariably start with are the characters. I map them out: I work out who they are, what their situation is, what wavelength they're on, how they relate to themselves and the people around them. As I build up a picture of the people I'm writing about, the setting begins to develop, too. From there the ideas come together naturally, and often very logically. So I don't start off with an entire story in mind—it grows over a period of time.

'The idea for the plot works from the character. For example, Trevor in *Cannily Cannily* is based on two actual children. In fact, most of the people I write about are kids and adults I've known and grown up with or continue to work with. One of the two children that I used as the basis for Trevor fired up a whole range of ideas that are presented in *Cannily Cannily*. This child, Sam, was in a country town where I was at college. He was very different in appearance and patterns of thought to the children he went to school with, and the ideas for the book really started because of this. Because I knew him and his mother well, and aspects of what he was going through were similar to some of my own experiences, I was able to put together a whole other range of ideas that was a quite natural extension of this character portrait—a rural setting, issues of conformity, organised childrens' sport, and so on.

'I piece the stories together like a jigsaw. Some incidents in my stories are entirely fictional, but by and large they've been lifted from real life.

'I was always an observer. As a child I didn't necessarily participate, but I certainly checked out what other kids did and said, how they worked together (or sometimes didn't work together) as a group. I think I've a lot by way of observational skills, and that power of observation leads on to me being able to really think as my characters think. I'd like to feel I can continue to develop these skills.

'I consciously think to myself, when I'm watching

someone or something, that whatever is being observed or overheard could develop into a storyline. While I was writing *Cannily Cannily*, I particularly tuned in to conservations between parents and kids in supermarkets or on the sidelines of childrens' football matches, as well as conversations in school staffrooms during my first prac teaching sessions.'

ALLAN BAILLIE

Allan Baillie began his writing career as a journalist, but in 1964 a sporting accident put him in a rehabilitation hospital for about a year and his career ideas changed. Travelling, working as a journalist, writing adult novels and short stories for children have all brought him to many themes that he wants to explore, and he now writes full-time.

'Ideas come from anywhere. The idea for *Adrift* came when my wife came into my office with a newspaper clipping that told of four boys and their dog drifting off from Beirut on a huge refrigerator case. They were in the water for a week. My wife said: "Can't you do something with this?" So then this idea started to change into what became the finished book.

'The idea for *Little Brother* came from meeting a boy in a border camp in Thailand. He told me how he escaped from the Khmer Rouge. I met several other people there, and about a year after I came home I suddenly realised that I had an excellent idea for a book.

'The idea for *Megan's Star* came from two or three sentences in a book which I was reading, called *The Atlas of World Mysteries*. I won't say where exactly, because if readers know where it's from, they'll know what I'm getting at. There's a very intriguing mystery there, so I thought why not work it out?

'One book came to me in a flash—at 1 o'clock in the

morning! It's a picture book called *Drac and the Gremlin*. It's a very simple idea, and it just wrote itself. The idea came from watching my kids playing in the backyard and remembering how I played, how I dramatised who I was pretending to be.

'I do remember things. I don't look out for things, wondering if I can use them to write a book. But sometimes in the future, what I've seen or remembered becomes an idea for a book. In *Adrift*, for example, I used an experience that's happened to me. I sail a lot, and sometimes I've been stuck out on Pittwater without any wind and no petrol in the tank—just drifting along. So, that feeling was easy to get into the book.

'There was also the terror of the children slowly drifting away from the shore and watching it going away. It happened to me, although not on a raft. I went swimming once late in the day. There was no one on the beach but a friend of mine, and I got caught in a rip. I could see the shore quietly sliding away, and my mate couldn't do anything. He just stood there, getting smaller and smaller. I used the memory of that feeling firstly in a short story called *The Rip*, and then the story became part of the book *Adrift*.

'Also in *Adrift* there was a cat who caught a crab. This did happen, but it wasn't a crab and it wasn't on the beach. A cat we had did carry on like a Persian king, but one afternoon it caught itself a frill-necked lizard by the tail, and the lizard caught the cat by the tail. Apparently the lizard could bite harder than the cat, and the cat dropped the lizard which didn't move a muscle. The cat kept on sniffing around looking for a moving lizard until finally it gave up, and then the lizard just walked away. The memory of that cat got in to my story, but I wasn't thinking that I could use the idea of the cat when it happened. What happens is that while writing, I might suddenly think: "Hey! That thought or that memory goes right there!"

'However, the idea comes first in writing a book, not the memory. Then the characters start taking shape, and that changes the story. The ideas, however, don't change.

'The only time an idea has changed is when I wrote *Little Brother*. I went to the Cambodian border looking for a book to write for adults. Then, while I was writing *Adrift*, I got the idea that my Cambodian book could be written as a children's book. I realised that this could be the way that I could write about Cambodia without having more of the horror of the real war in it than the reader could bear.'

ROBERT CORMIER

Like Simon French, Robert Cormier also began writing when he was young—he was just thirteen. For Robert Cormier, being able to write is a 'little secret joy' that he carries around with him, despite the dramatic and sometimes frightening ideas that concern him which appear in books like *The Chocolate War* and *I Am the Cheese*.

'I launch a book usually through an emotion. I'm a very emotional writer. I don't dream up a plot by saying: "Oh, I think I'll write a hijacking story." Or: "Gee—government abuse of privacy is in the headlines today, I think I'll write a story about that." I don't do that.

'Usually something happens to me and I become emotionally involved, and then I create a character and put the character into a situation that's current, and on my mind. I have themes—things that I'm interested in—and they're almost a thread through my writing. So, when something happens and I have an emotional response to it, I start evolving a character. I'll then put that character into a situation that reflects my fears about things that are going on in the world today, from terrorism, to being given numbers for everything.'

LEE HARDING
Like Robert Cormier, author Lee Harding also begins to write from a strong feeling.

'I think all writers are observant. Writers are people who look closely at life. If I'm at a restaurant I make sure I have a corner table with my back to the wall. If I get on a tram I automatically sit up the far end. It's not that I'm consciously looking at people and making notes, but I don't want to miss anything. You need to be an observer and to really notice things.

'I think I'm an "unconscious" writer. I really don't make notes. I really don't plot very much in writing. I'd find that tedious and boring. I generally start with a number of characters and a strong feeling or theme, and the book grows organically out of that. Very often I don't know what I'm going to write until I sit down. And I figure if I don't know what I'm going to put on a page, the reader won't know either and will keep turning the page!

'*Displaced Person* came about because I got sick and tired of waiting to be served. I then asked myself the great "What if" question: "What if someone was ignored out of existence?" And that became my theme.

'My themes arise out of a strong feeling—something I feel intensely about. Once I have my theme, the plot evolves out of the characters. If I only write out of what I know, then other people can know the same things and it could be a bit boring. But if I write out of what I feel, only I can feel that way and this is the beginning of style and the writer's individual voice.'

CYNTHIA VOIGT
'Usually some particular thing happens which gives me an idea for a story, and it's never the same thing. The idea for *Homecoming* began when I went to the supermarket one day and had a stray thought. I parked

in the parking lot, and, as I was walking down to the supermarket I saw some kids waiting in a car. As I walked through the door the thought struck me: "What if nobody comes back for those kids?"

'Another book idea was a dream, I think. Some ideas come out of other ones. As I'm writing one story I know what the next one's going to be. There's usually some particular point where the book idea starts, but it's usually so *buried* back there in time.

'I travel with pieces of paper, and I have an ideas notebook because I think that when I run dry I'll flip back through it and see what's there. Then I tend to forget about the idea, and my theory is if I forget about it it's probably not a very good idea, and there are a lot of those in my ideas notebook.

'But if I can't forget about it, and I've not only written it down but I've written down subsequent ideas that I've had because it won't go away, then I know it's something I've got to get around to writing, when I feel like it. That can be some time later.'

MICHAEL DUGAN

Michael Dugan left school determined to become a writer. But when his first two books were rejected by every publisher he sent them to, it didn't seem to be a very promising start. However, his first book was published while he was working in a bookshop in Melbourne, and since then he's never looked back.

'In my nonsense verses the idea might come very quickly—just from seeing a word, and another which rhymes with it. A book might be quite different and happen over a long period of time.

'For example, *Dingo Boy* came basically from three events which occurred over a period of about ten years, and it wasn't until the third of these events occurred that

I got the idea of combining all three into one book. The first experience came from working in a children's home when I was in my late teens, and I heard stories of children who'd been fostered on to farms and hadn't liked it and had run away. The second came about five years later, when I was staying in the Flinders Ranges and heard and saw and learnt a bit about dingoes. And the third was the geographical setting, which came when I helped my retired parents move from the city to the country.

'It was looking at the little range of hills behind their new home, and thinking that if there were dingoes in those hills then the farmers would have to build dingo-proof fences around them, which really brought home the idea for the book. It would be about a boy fostered on to a farm, into an uncaring family more interested in him as free labour than as a person, and the boy identifying with dingoes and their struggle for existence and freedom. It would be about him growing away from the farm environment and eventually planning his escape.

'Mostly, it's situations which spark off the idea for one of my books, but in this case it was my memory of the fostered children.

'I keep a diary, and also make notes of ideas and keep them in a file, for they might be useful some time. For a long time I've looked and listened as a writer, although I've not deliberately tried to do this. I don't tend to write down conversations that I've had, although I might write down a phrase that I've heard—especially if I've heard something fairly striking. Generally, I've got a good memory for conversation. These fragments can be a source of a story, but more often they're the ways in which I keep up with how people, especially children, talk. In particular, it helps me with the expressions they use.'

ROBERT LEESON

Like Michael Dugan, Robert Leeson's ideas for stories can grow over many years.

'The first thing to do is to avoid looking at an empty page, and to let a story start in your own mind. The worst thing you can do is to rush at it and try and write the whole story down. Once you get an idea you want to chew it over like a bit of toffee for a while, and it can be chewed over in your mind for a long long time.

'The original idea for *The Third Class Genie* came to me when I was ten years old. I was standing on a bridge over the canal thinking of going for a walk, and I spotted a tin can in the gutter. I kicked it all the way down the hill and at the bottom of the hill, in a drum yard, somebody shouted out. I thought they were shouting at me so I ran off along the canal. Then I slowed up and I realised he was shouting at somebody else. As I walked along I began to think . . . supposing the Invisible Man had been having a kip inside the can and I kicked him all the way down the hill, and that was *him* shouting at me? And that was as far as it went.

'That was the idea, and I think that when you get an idea like that the best thing to do is treasure it for a bit, and eventually other possibilities will come to you to extend that idea, and you can feel the idea growing in your mind. That's when you *know* you are on to a story. I've learnt to use a notebook simply to put down these ideas as they come to me, and to keep on adding to them in the notebook.

'So that's really the first stage, with nothing written, no blank sheet of paper, just an idea growing in the mind. And the next stage is to work out the plot of the story.'

Historical Fiction

ROSEMARY SUTCLIFF

Rosemary Sutcliff had to have many operations when she was a child. After a long break she found herself facing one more, and felt miserable, lonely and scared. She wanted somebody to keep her company while she waited to have the operation, and out of that need came Marcus, the hero of her first book, *The Eagle of the Ninth*.

'Ideas sometimes come very obviously from having read an article in a magazine, or something that somebody has said. Sometimes one just apparently comes in the window of its own accord. Sometimes I really only get the idea that I want to write a story with a certain background and, little by little, the characters will emerge from the background.

'I think *The Lantern Bearers* was one of the most dramatic arrivals really. That really did walk in through the window when I was trying to make some toast, and I suddenly thought out of nowhere: "Yes, but when the Roman legions were withdrawn from Britain, they'd been here over 400 years. That's the same time as between us and the first Queen Elizabeth! They didn't go home on leave. They got married where they were posted, so they must all have been practically British by birth."

'I wondered how many of them just went wilfully missing, and never went back with the legions because Britain was their home, and not Rome. And then I started from there to produce *The Lantern Bearers*.

'But mostly it isn't as dramatic as that. It comes from somewhere, but I have to wait around for it, poke around for it, and think a lot first.'

Poetry

JACK PRELUTSKY

Jack Prelutsky says he collects the ideas that inspire his funny and sometimes zany poems by being aware of the world about him.

'Ideas are very valuable, whether it's a word or an abstract idea. They're what makes it possible for me to write. I never know ahead of time which idea coming into my mind is going to be the most valuable, so I always carry a notebook with me and I write down everything. It doesn't matter what. If someone tells me a stupid pickle joke, or if an odd rhyme comes into my mind, or if I see a man who's six feet eight and he's got a penguin on his head and he's wearing purple socks, I write that down. They're all just grab shots, like the photographs I'm always taking, and it happens so quickly I don't really judge if they're worth anything or not. That comes later. Only about ten per cent of all those things that go into a notebook ever surface as poems. But I can't decide what I'm going to use until later.

'I write down an idea, and that idea may be a pickle joke. It leads to two other ideas, which might lead to four other ideas each. Some of these are dead ends, and some keep on growing. By writing down the original idea, you can't predict where it might eventually lead you.

'Ideas come because I am a human being who is aware of the world. And I'm aware of the world in a certain way. For example, let's say there's a four-year-old kid out there on a street with his puppy, who's having a great time with a fire hydrant which is on. Now, if I'm walking by and I'm a barber, I'll notice that the kid could use a haircut. If I'm walking by and I'm a veterinarian, I'll wonder if the dog has had its shots.

If I'm a fireman, I'll wonder why the fire hydrant is turned on.

'But I happen to be walking by as a poet, and I'll say: this is a wonderful idea for a poem.

'Ideas come from everything that happens to us. They come because we are humans, and if we are aware humans it's impossible not to have ideas.

'I've trained myself to be the sort of person to notice all these things in this way. I always had an active, vivid imagination, which helped to keep me alive in the particular neighbourhood where I grew up. You see, in order to survive there you had to be one of four things. You had to be either big and strong and a good fighter, or you had to be friends with someone who was big and strong and a good fighter—or you had to be a fast runner. Or, barring all those things, you had to be a fast talker, and I was a fast talker. I got out of a lot of situations because I talked my way out, and to do that you have to use your imagination. So I've trained myself. Now, when I've finished a book of poems, I wind up with more ideas than when I started. Ideas breed ideas, and the more you start using your eyes and your ears and your brain and your heart, the more ideas happen.'

EVE MERRIAM

The idea for Eve Merriam's first book of children's poems came from being told that there was no rhyme for the words 'silver' and 'orange'. She invented a rhyme for silver, and called the collection of rhyming poems *There Is No Rhyme for Silver.* **She then wrote her second collection of children's poems which she called** *It Doesn't Always Have to Rhyme.*

'Sometimes an idea for a poem will come with a word that I've found. I love to play around with language, so if I come across an unusual word that strikes me as amusing or something one can bounce to, I think: "Well now! That would be fun to play around with." If I get that kind of idea, then generally it will be a poem that rhymes, because the rhymes themselves are fun to play around with. It's like playing a game where you have rules to go by.

'I once came across the world "ululation". I thought: "Ululation! I don't know what this means." So I went to the dictionary and I looked it up, and it meant "uttering cries". I thought that was a wonderful idea, so I made a poem called "Ululation". The whole poem consisted of the way various creatures give out with sounds like "baa-aa", or "squeak", and I described all of the birds and the animals and the sounds that they made, so it was all built around that word.

'Then sometimes there will be some thing that strikes me. I used to live on the upper West Side in New York, overlooking the Hudson River, and it was a very beautiful place with trees, and the shimmer of the river and the sky. In front of the apartment where I lived there was a car that had been abandoned. It was getting rustier and rustier, and it wasn't even worthwhile for a junk dealer to come and tow it away.

'That made me think of things like plastic bottles that just don't disintegrate. And so I began to imagine what it would be like at the end of the world, when all of our bodies had become dust, but plastic bottles and all these beat-up cars were still there. What a strange picture!

'So I carried this notion around for a long time and I finally called the poem "Landscape". It dealt with a landscape in the future, and the first line began: "What will you find at the edge of the world?" Not the "end" of the world, because I thought of the world as an edge with all these objects that were just falling off, and maybe just one thing would be left to remind us of what our civilisation had been, a junkyard of cars.

'So the idea for this poem came in the opposite way

to the idea for "Ululation", where I was dealing with language first. This idea for a landscape of the future came from something I saw outside my window.'

Non-Fiction

SEYMOUR SIMON

Because he was once a science teacher, the ideas for many of Seymour Simon's books arise out of his own curiosity about what he sees and experiences around him.

'Getting an idea for a book can come from anywhere. I've written a number of books about computers which came about as a result of buying a computer and simply using it myself, but it was years after getting the computer that it occurred to me that there might be a book in it. Sometimes I'll see a photograph that just ignites my imagination, and I can think of a whole book where I can use that photograph as a taking-off place.

'So the ideas can come from anywhere, but the crucial thing to realise that deciding to do a book about the subject is not really good enough. What I have to do is have a particular point of view. I decide that I want to give my own personal voice to the subject and present it in a way which hasn't been presented before. I wrote a book called *The Paper Airplane Book* so that aeroplanes could be used as a method to teach something about the principles of air — that was my real idea, not just paper aeroplanes.

'I keep an ideas file. It's even labelled "Writing Ideas", but it's just a jog to my memory, full of jotted down notes to remind me about ideas I might have had while reading the paper or watching television. I get my book ideas from anything that interests me. It doesn't happen the other way round. I don't decide to write a book and then look around for a subject to write on.'

GETTING READY TO WRITE

Very few writers can begin to write without having spent time thinking about the development of their story. There are exceptions though, and Sue Townsend is one. Here writers describe the various ways in which their ideas change and develop over time, as they get ready to write.

Picture Books

MICHAEL FOREMAN

'I know that I have, in my sketchbooks, ideas for places where I'd like to set a story. When the germ of an idea for a story makes its appearance, the next stage is to refer back to my sketchbooks, and then I draw little sketches for each page. By doing these I can see how much of the story can be told only in pictures, and how much of the story has to be told with text. I then use the words to thread the various pictures together, and that becomes my plan.

'My ideas for pictures come first, and then I think about how I am going to use my text to link them.

'If I can't think of a last line for my book, I don't start. I should be able to see my story from beginning to end. Then I keep working on an outline of the text, which

is done at the same time as the little picture scribbles.
I am rethinking the pictures and reshaping the text as
I go along.'

Humour

SUE TOWNSEND

'I don't plan anything. All I know, when I set out to write
anything at all, is the sort of tone, the sort of atmosphere,
and the sort of feeling that I want the reader to get. I
don't know how I'm going to achieve that. I don't know
what the story is going to be. I'm just after an
atmosphere, a tone and a voice.

'I start at the beginning and write in the order of the
story. The characters just take off and live their own
lives although, of course, I'm guiding them and
manipulating them. But I don't know what's going to
happen.'

THOMAS ROCKWELL

'Writing is really a process of getting one idea after
another. For example, with *How to Eat Fried Worms*,
it's fairly easy to write about the first worm that the boy
eats, because it is such a funny disgusting thing to do.
And then I wrote the same thing for the next worm and
realised that I couldn't keep doing that throughout the
book, because it would get dull.

'So then I had to think up all sorts of other, different
things that could happen — still connected to the book
idea, but which would be funny and interesting. To be
able to do this sort of thing, I think I'm the sort of person
who notices everything. Anybody who wants to write
anything has to be an observer.

'However, I don't think up all these sorts of things
before I write the first word of my story. I usually don't
make an outline, because I only have an idea of where
I'm going and that will change as I write. I really don't

know how I want the book to finish. The ideas come to me as I go along. They may not be as large an idea as the main one, but they have to be just as interesting, and they have to move the book at a good pace.'

BEVERLY CLEARY

'I don't keep notebooks, other than a composition book with a few words or phrases in it. Sometimes I completely forget what they were for. I find it's more important to keep all these stray bits of ideas and rubbish tumbling around in my mind. An author's mind is a little bit like a scrap bag. If I want something I can usually rummage around and find it.

'I usually think about a book for three years before I begin to write. I thought of *Ramona the Pest* for fifteen years before I began to write it. I have to mull the story over and let it begin to take on a life of its own.

'I think about whether it's a good idea. Will I enjoy writing it? Then, once I have a general idea of the story, I begin to collect information and ideas from the world around me. I'll overhear a shred of conversation which I think will fit, or read something in the newspaper which will fit. I don't write an outline, because I can't make it work in writing fiction. I just have to let the story grow.

'When I start a book, I take an exercise book and I pretend that there are going to be ten chapters in the book, although it doesn't necessarily turn out that way. I set up tentative ideas, and as I write and the characters grow, I jot down in each chapter a few words or a few phrases which may or may not turn up in the book.'

MAX DANN

'I spend about a week drawing up a plan of what I'm going to write—as much as I possibly can. I find that if it doesn't come after that amount of time, then I become impatient and I'll begin writing. Actually, the story really starts to happen to me when I start writing, anyway.

'Usually I have an idea of how the story is going to end before I start, but I rarely use that same ending, or even my planned plot. I don't expect to use it either. It's just the basis or skeleton on which I start, and I know it's going to change, once I start writing.

'I always write the first drafts in longhand — it's very old-fashioned. I usually write the first draft straight through, and then start again and rewrite it.'

Fantasy

VICTOR KELLEHER

'From all those bits and pieces of ideas that I get from reading books, listening to people, going to the movies, dreaming, and all the rest of it, sooner or later I'll take one of those ideas which feels like a kind of a nerve centre. I know it's going to be the centre of the book because it's a good idea which kind of flares for me.

'I never put pen to paper, I don't even make much in the way of notes, until a kind of structure begins to form in my head. That can take weeks or months — it can even take years — but there comes a point when I know that I can write up a kind of synopsis, or bits of a synopsis which are nearly always trials, and I do that. I sit down and usually do that on a typewriter (although I normally write longhand) because it makes me put one word after another.

'I try to write — if not a synopsis of the whole book, then bits and pieces of it — in very, very brief outline. They're just ideas, and may be only a page or two of writing. That forces me to recognise all the gaps and all the bits that don't work. It isolates pieces of the puzzle (because the puzzle can sprawl in any direction) and it enables me to single out those areas that I want to think about.

'And then I think about them. I think about them while I'm at work, or while I'm running or sitting around with my family. My family says that that's when I'm buzzing, because I sit around and I talk to myself, especially when I'm writing. I mumble, because I wrestle with ideas by wrestling with sentences, and vice versa. That process starts when I'm actually trying to put it together in my head.

'I don't start to write until I have a working structure. I know where I want to start, and I have to know where I'm going to finish. But I must add that, in the writing process, that structure bends and undergoes all kinds of strains, and sometimes breaks apart, but I still have to start with a structure. However, the trick in writing a good book is to not be totally held by that structure. The structure is there to allow me to know roughly where I'm going, so that I can work on the language and the rhythm and the "artistic" side of the writing.

'I know that I'm not going to sit down and write, until I have what I would call "World" in my head. This isn't only an imaginary space and place, but it has a very real time scheme and it has sequence.'

'There is an outline or a plan in my head. I don't write it down because that sets it. But I have to have a plan because there has to be something that can be changed. You can't start out with nothing, and have nothing changed into something. But if you start with a plan, then there's something that can be changed.'

Madeleine L'Engle

Realistic Fiction and Adventure Stories

LEE HARDING

'I find it important to visualise my first scene before I sit down to start writing. I'll go through a ream of paper trying to get the first page right, because that first page will set my style, my atmosphere—the whole development will spring from that first page. I don't like to work out where I'm going. I have a vague idea of an ending in my mind, not written down anywhere, and the middle bit always muddles itself out.

'I'm a very slow worker, about 500 words a day. And I've probably mulled the ideas over for a year or so, because I find that one book leads into another. I might be halfway through writing one book, and I'll begin to get a theme, or vague images or ideas, for the next one. Even though it may take me two or three years to work on one book, there's always the next book forming in my head at the same time.

'I know that I'm ready to start writing because I just can't put it off for any longer. I have to begin this book. Writing is very hard work, and I put it off by doing other pleasurable things, but there comes a time when I have to start writing, so that it can grow and become a book. I have to get something concrete down on paper. It's more important to have errors to correct, than to have a blank page. You can only think about doing something for so long. Then you have to say: "Right. This is page one." And get on with it!'

SIMON FRENCH

'I really do piece the story together like a jigsaw, before I start to write. In thinking about the people in the story, I'll scribble down notes relating to that person I'm writing about. It might be little "streams of consciousness" things that the character is thinking over or, by contrast, other peoples' views of that character.

'Having written ideas down on paper, I'll shuffle them around a fair bit. The storyline thus comes together, sometimes over a fairly long period of time. The storyline for *Hey, Phantom Singlet* took a couple of years to come together, which was partly due to my being at school at the time and having to fit it in with schoolwork. *Cannily Cannily* took about six months for the storyline to fall into place, but I then spent about another year ordering the story correctly and working at the sort of "style" I was aiming for.'

ALLAN BAILLIE

'Location might suggest a book. For example, in *Eagle Island*, I knew what I wanted to use a deserted island in the Whitsundays, where I'd been for a holiday. I thought about the villains perhaps planning to do something dreadful on the Great Barrier Reef. I was going to put the boy on this island, and the villains going there. How? Well, perhaps their boat breaks down and is sinking.

However, at this point in my thinking, I realised that this story sounded just like any other adventure story, and I needed to make it a bit more complicated. When I thought about the boy sailing his catamaran across to the island by himself, I realised that, often, children with handicaps are allowed by their parents to do extraordinary things. If the boy was handicapped, it might make it more believable that he'd be allowed to do these sorts of things. So, new ideas started to weave together.

'I think all of this out before I begin to write. These thoughts are all a sort of stew in my head. I'd only occasionally jot down very few notes. If it's a good thought, it will quietly muddle away and stay with me. Then I'd start seeking out information I might need and making notes about that for myself.

'It takes different amounts of time to think all these things out and be ready to start writing. I thought up *Adrift* in about two days, and then wrote the first and second drafts in three months. I then slowed down and completed it in about seven months. With *Riverman*, it took about twelve or thirteen years for the idea to surface.'

ROBERT CORMIER

'I outline my story in my mind, but I don't write this outline down. I know where my story is going to, but I'm not quite sure what's going to happen along the way. I let my characters take me towards the climax of the story. Sometimes I'll introduce a new character, and if it doesn't work I'll dump them, or just leave them in for one chapter. I write towards a destination, but as I write I'm looking for a climax.

'An example of how this occurs can be seen in my novel *The Chocolate War*. I knew that in this book the climax had to be a confrontation between the good guys and the bad guys, Jerry Reynold and Archie Costello, and so I was working towards that. I didn't know what it would be at the time, but I knew there was a strong element of boxing in the story. So, before I began, I knew the climax would be physical and probably some kind of boxing match. I went on to write the novel along these lines.

'The story is always on my mind. The characters become so real to me, and I'm so involved with them, that they are with me all the time. I'm a night person. I stay up very late at night and, invariably, I'm thinking incessantly about my writing.'

CYNTHIA VOIGT

'Sometimes when I have an idea for a book I do better to sit on the idea for a year or two, and let it sort of grow.

However, I have written a couple of books fairly close to when I got the original idea. No book is ever really the same for me. The really nice ones come in and take over, and I barely have to think about those. I just sort of wallow in them for however long it takes to write them.

'The shortest time this thinking process has taken for me is when I stewed about something for a couple of weeks, and then wrote it.

'I know how I'm going to end my story before I begin to write. I don't know the exact words and situations. I have to discover what I want to say. Last lines and first lines give me a lot of trouble. Deep in the middle is what tends to go easily — unless it's going badly, in which case it is the worst of the lot.

'I don't know clearly what events are going to occur in the story. I try to find a feeling for event in the first chapter and I show it to myself. Things become clearer to me after I've written a couple of chapters, and then those ideas create other ideas of what I'm going to do. So, I start with an outline notebook that has a sort of chapter plan.

'On each facing half page I'll write in ideas that crossed my mind as I started writing from the chapter plan, and which I might want to work into the story. In another part of the notebook, I'll put in parts of ideas for further on in the book which doesn't have a specific outline yet. These ideas are the beginning of the specific outline for later in the book, and they've come because of what I've been writing at the beginning.

'So, my notebook is a kind of living document, growing as I'm writing the book. All the pages are coded, and I also write in the back of it, working on what I call "long-line thoughts" — ideas that I want to run through the whole story.'

ROBERT LEESON

'The first stage of the book has nothing written, just an idea growing in the mind. It's a pity not to allow enough time for this growing process to happen. When I was a lad and I first tried to write novels, I'd find that after the first two or three chapters I'd run out of puff. I couldn't think of anything else to write. Adult writers call it "writer's block". Now I know that I have to be patient and allow the story to grow in my mind until I'm quite certain that I know how it's going to go.

'The next stage for me is to work out the plot of the story. The plot of the story is like a skeleton, and the description, the characters and all the rest of it are the body. When I feel that I've got enough ideas I spend a lot of time (several weeks at a time) working out the plot in the very greatest detail. I never actually start writing a story until I'm just about certain of everything that's going to happen.

'While I'm making the plot, I get a huge piece of paper and down the left-hand side I put the names of all the characters. Sometimes they may be worked out in great detail. Sometimes they may just be "person", "boy", or "girl", and I might not have even given them a name. And then, across the sheet of paper, I put down what's going to happen to each character in the course of that story, just in little notes.

'So, I set down everything that's going to be in the story, in note form, on one sheet of paper, so that I can look at it. It's important to get all these ideas in my mind out, so that I can look at them.'

MICHAEL DUGAN

'The first thing I do to start writing is to make a chapter-by-chapter outline. These are just rough headings, because at this stage of writing I can't make a substantial outline.

'Then I make a fairly tight point-by-point summary

of how the story is going to go, and construct a chapter synopsis. I've definitely thought out how it's going to start, what the middle is, and what my ending is going to be.

'I also make notes on my characters because it's embarrassing if they change hair colouring, or something, halfway through. These notes are descriptions of them, and some ideas about their lives before the events of my book took place. This gives me a firm picture of each character to build on, even though this information is for myself, and doesn't usually go into the book.

'Altogether I have about twelve pages of notes, and I'm ready to begin writing when I've finished my point-by-point synopsis of a book. Only then can I feel reasonably confident that it's going to work.'

Historical Fiction

ROSEMARY SUTCLIFF

'I get a feeling that I want to write about a particular place and a particular period, and I sort of sit and brew on that and see what emerges. Often the characters then step out of that place and period.

'I then get a large red exercise book and start to do my research. I copy everything down on to the backs of envelopes and then, if I don't lose the envelopes, I put them all into my red exercise book in groups, one page to each idea or piece of information. Now I've got everything together under one roof.

'When I've got it all together, then I start writing the story. The book is fairly well shaped in my mind before I begin writing. It isn't a detailed synopsis, but I know the beginning, middle and end. I just can't start writing a book and think I'll find out how it ends later. I've got to know how it ends. Usually my idea of what the story is going to be about and what is going to happen in it start emerging at the same time. The two things run side by side.'

Poetry

JACK PRELUTSKY

'I was in my local supermarket one day, shopping for supper, and I decided to get some boneless breasts of chicken. Suddenly I thought: "What about the rest of the chicken? Was it boneless too? Did it have a calcium deficiency?" I thought it might be interesting to write about a boneless chicken, so I wrote this down in my notebook straight away. Idea: Boneless Chicken.

'I do this immediately, because unless you take advantage of an idea straight away, something else takes its place. I go through my notebook when I get back home to my studio, and I transfer my idea to the word processor.

'I know it's going to be a nonsense poem, because if I'm constructing a world in which a boneless chicken can live, then it's a nonsense poem.

'I'll tell you a terrific secret about writing nonsense. A lot of people think that nonsense is easy to write because you can just start with, for example:

"The purple swarm went out with the green gazzoop
And they sat under an orange gabooka tree . . ."

and it doesn't mean anything because there are no rules. But, for nonsense poems to really work, I have to make a framework. I create an artificial world which works only for the purposes of this poem, but I make sure that everything I say in this poem, even though it's nonsense, works within that framework.

'I start by pre-writing. I extend the idea of the boneless chicken. The first thing I say to myself is: "Yes, there *is* such a thing as a boneless chicken." So I ask serious questions about that chicken. They're the basic, who, what, where, how, when, why questions I'd ask about anything. I'd also add a few other questions: why not? what if? supposing . . .? I don't ask silly questions.

'I write down what I think would be reasonable answers to these questions, and then puzzle over a way to lead to the end of the poem. It's simple with a poem about a chicken, because I can bring the poem full circle with answering a question about what sort of egg would a boneless chicken lay.

'I came up with a few answers on this: the boneless egg, obviously, and soft-boiled was a possibility.'

Non-Fiction

SEYMOUR SIMON

'I don't write a plan, but there's always an outline in my mind. I always know what I'm going to be doing. I frequently put an outline on paper, but it's very rough because it changes considerably as I work on something.

'I think about the whole idea of how I'm going to do the book—the approach I'm going to take is much more important than actually getting the words down. For example, there are lots of books written about dinosaurs. The ones where the writer has just pulled out facts from encyclopaedias, and then written to order, are the ones which are really rather boring. I think for a long time about the particular point of view I'm going to write from so that, hopefully, this does not happen in my books.'

RESEARCH

Research is obviously very important to writers of historical fiction like Rosemary Sutcliff, and non-fiction writers like Seymour Simon. But many other authors find that they either cannot begin writing until they have carried out some research, or that they need to look for more information once they have begun a story.

ROSEMARY SUTCLIFF

'I do do my homework. I do a lot of research, and in some cases it's a really big job to get all the things researched before I start writing. I collect the material that I need. I write to people and ask them questions about gunnery or horses or whatever it is I need to know.

'I don't always go to the place that I'm writing about, and some of my best-written locations are places I've never actually been to. I read up on them from guidebooks and country histories, from histories of the flora and fauna of a place, and the books that people write about a place when they've been on a walking tour of it. I read anything that has got the atmosphere of the place and the wildlife. Then I put them all together. I find that when I've read enough books like these about a place, I discover that they have a centre where they all seem to meet. And this is my key to the place I'm writing about.

'Then, while I'm writing, I keep on finding other things that I haven't found out about, so I keep having panics all the way through the writing. When that happens, I stop writing and find out what I need.'

SEYMOUR SIMON

Because he writes non-fiction, research is also essential to Seymour Simon.

'The amount of research varies widely with each book that I write. *Hidden Worlds: Pictures of the Invisible* took years to get photographs from many different places, and then to decide what I wanted to do with those photographs once I'd got them.

'The research for *The Paper Airplane Book* came out of some experiments I did with kids at school, just before they started a project on air. I told them that I wanted them to go home and make the best paper aeroplane they could, and bring it in to school the next day.

'Then we had a paper aeroplane flying contest to see which planes went the highest, which went the longest distance, which did the best loops. We even had a prize for the handsomest plane, chosen from the ones that couldn't fly. Afterwards we discussed why the planes flew the way that they did. We talked about experiments and we asked "What if" questions. What if we added paperclips? Would that help the plane to fly? Where would we put the paperclips? How do we know?

'This was my research. I had hundreds of models that had been made, and I had to look through them all and choose what I wanted to use. After doing all of this research, I started writing the book.'

'Sometimes I have to do research for my stories, though I try to avoid it if I can. I usually know enough of my story in advance to know if it needs some information researched, but I usually avoid writing about things I don't know about. I think it's better to write about things with which you are as familiar as possible.'

Max Dann

BEVERLY CLEARY

'If I have to do any research for my stories, I do it during the writing of the book, as well as having the manuscript checked at the end. One story I wrote had a Harley-Davidson motorcycle in it, and while I was writing it I went to a motorcycle shop and asked questions, and I studied safety manuals and driving instruction codes. Then the manuscript was sent to the Harley-Davidson office in New York, who went over it very carefully and made some recommendations so that it would be accurate.

'When I wrote *Dear Mr Henshaw*, which has a truck-driving father in it, I had to do some research on trucking in California. I'd written part of the book and I could see that I needed to know more about trucks than I actually did. I went to a truck saleyard and looked at trucks, and talked to some very dusty looking characters who found my questions very amusing. I knew that I wanted to climb into the cab of a truck and see what it was like, which is what I did.'

'It's very important for me to have been to the places that I'm drawing. I need to have spent time in these countries and I need to know the people. This puts something extra and original into my illustrations, instead of having to use material from the reference library like many illustrators have to do.'

Michael Foreman

ALLAN BAILLIE

'I do research information or feeling or character for my books. When I was writing *Eagle Island*, which has a very independent deaf boy as the main character, I set up a meeting with two deaf boys and their parents. One of the boys sailed a sailboard, and his father told me about his one terror at realising, as he watched his son sailing out, that he couldn't call him back. That idea went into the book.

'I also always get hold of experts and use them. One expert working with deaf children put me in touch with a boy who was also a very good mime artist, and what he showed me about being a mime artist went into the book.

'I spent a month in Tasmania researching ideas for *Riverman*, and ended up with great wads of information. I wrote the book and submitted it to the publishers who said: "Congratulations on the research, Allan, but what about the plot!" So, I rewrote it.'

'While writing fiction, I try to do as much research as I will need before I commence writing. However this rarely works out, and I find I need to research new aspects, or research more deeply, as I go along.'

Michael Dugan

LLOYD ALEXANDER

'I do a lot of research for my stories before I start to write the first draft. In the story about the cat, called *Time Cat*, I read every book about cats that I could find. When I found something interesting I'd think: "Ah! This is good. I'll use this, somehow."

'I'd then make a note of what I'd found. For each episode of his nine lives, I actually did hard serious research on the historical period of that particular country.

'But when I'm ready to write, I must forget it and throw the research away. By now I must have absorbed my research so thoroughly that it becomes second nature, and then it will really work for me. The researched information will weave naturally into the story. It's awful when the research shows in a story, because it hasn't become a natural part of the writing.'

CHARACTERS AND SETTINGS

Picture Books

'The basic character in many of my books is me, particularly in the Frog and Toad books. I also base many of my characters on friends of mine.

'I sympathise with all my characters, even though they may not be terribly pleasant. I don't think I've ever really created a terrible villian.'

Arnold Lobel

STEVEN KELLOGG

'My characters come from inside me, usually. They also come from fragments of things and people, and experiences that I've had. I just use lots of different pieces of things that seem right and put them all together to create a character.

'Some of the characters are lifted directly from life. Pinkerton was like that. I got Pinkerton as a puppy ten years ago, and he was a shock! He was wonderful, but he was so stubborn and perverse and crazy and impossible to train. Yet, somehow he was so innocent in the middle of all his destructive qualities that he was totally lovable and irresistible. I was so struck by him that I started off writing the Pinkerton books.

'The children in my books mostly come from the child within me. Also, I grew up in a neighbourhood with lots of children. It was like a huge family that was a street long. So the faces and the personalities of the children in my books are drawn from these memories.

'I always take notice of people around me to use in my stories. I feel like I'm always doing my homework. If I'm talking to children I'm always watching their expressions, the way they sit, their movements, and the way they mix with each other as they come into a room. I watch adults as well — teachers, librarians and adult friends. I'm constantly recording in my mind what I see, and then I use little pieces of that (if they fit) in my illustrations or a piece of writing.

'I don't think I could create a character I didn't really like. I would probably be bored and offended by it. But I think that villains can be lovable and exciting, and can make the story move more quickly. Dr Kibble, for example, in the Pinkerton books, is so stuffy and bossy and awful, and yet I'm very fond of her.'

SUE TOWNSEND

'My characters are all the people I've ever observed or met. I worked in youth groups for thirteen years, and I worked in adventure playgrounds and community homes for old people, so I've seen all the characters in my books. My stepfather is a postman and he's a very distinctive sort of person. He doesn't wear a bow tie like Courtney Elliot, the postman in *The Growing Pains of Adrian Mole*, but he takes big philosophical books to work, so I just extended that idea of him into my character.

'I don't sit down and compile a list of characters before I start work. They all just come down to me, even with their names. I can't write a character until they've got a name. Their name has to be exactly right. I'm very fond of names that seem to describe the person. You wouldn't know that Courtney Elliot is a postman, but you sort of get the taste of him from his name.

'The thing about characters is that you have to give them their own style. I also write plays, and it helps being a playwright because I know how to use speech to give a very good idea of what a character is like. It helps to instantly characterise them.'

ROBIN KLEIN

Here Robin Klein describes how Penny Pollard's character evolved.

'I knew the kind of character I wanted to write about. I knew that she was a strong little girl who was a bit of a misfit—a bit of a loner. I used to admire girls who were like Penny, whose personalities were very strong. I was such a wimpy little girl when I was growing up, and I had a cousin who was a bit like Penny. Nothing seemed to bother her either, and she had a solution for everything. I also grew up with horses and so it seemed natural that this character would like horses, too.

'Penny has now evolved into such a character in her own right, for me, that I know the sorts of things she'd like; what she'd be interested in. I even know what sort of books she'd have on the table beside her bed. The more I write about her, the more things about her character come out. I'm trying to develop her, but I don't want her to grow older than about eleven or twelve.

'I can see that there will be a time when I perhaps won't want to go on writing about Penny. I'm finding it harder to go back and recapture Penny, and all the characters and situations around her, after leaving her to go on and write other things. But she's very popular and children seem to get a lot from her, so there are more experiences with Penny in store.'

'My characters come from all sorts of different places. Some are people I knew as a kid, some are children I observed around me later on. When I was first writing, I'd try to listen to and work out how people talked. But now I find that I've just sort of soaked it up and I don't have to think about it too much.'

Thomas Rockwell

BEVERLY CLEARY

'My characters come from both what I've seen and what I've imagined. Henry Huggins is really a composite of some boys I knew in school when I was growing up. In early childhood, I was very much like Ramona, but once I started school I quickly turned into Ellen Tebbits, the most autobiographical of my characters.

'My characters change and develop as I write. Ramona appeared in only one paragraph in my book *Henry Huggins*. She was there to explain Beezus' unusual nickname. Also I wanted some of the children to have a sister or a brother. However, she kept turning up in the Henry books, and she grew until I was getting letters saying please write a whole book about Ramona. I began to think about it, and when my own twins began kindergarten and I found out all about the perils of starting school, I was able to write *Ramona the Pest*.'

MAX DANN

'The characters develop the story, and I think all of them may have come from people I've known or met sometime. But that doesn't mean I can select one person I know and then put them straight down on paper as they are. Rarely do you find a real character strong enough for that. I mix and blend.

'Each character I create is a melting pot of various people and their peculiarities — with always a slice of myself thrown in to help me understand how they think.'

Fantasy

VICTOR KELLEHER

'I never borrow my characters from life. No character of mine has ever stepped off the street and on to the page. They've always developed out of the "World" of the story.

'I may borrow people's names, and perhaps change them a bit, because names can be a problem.

'However, I do work from real places, even in my fantasy books. My fantasy landscapes are usually based on a conglomeration of real landscapes. I don't start to write about them until I've put my feet on them. And if I haven't done that for a long time, then if it's at all possible I like to walk over them and make notes before I start to write. Sometimes I know of the landscape I want to use, and sometimes I have to go looking for the right landscape. This is probably the most important research I do for a book, and I may travel long miles to find it. When I was writing *Taronga* I made many many visits to the zoo, over a long period of time.

'I take a great deal of notice of the detail of a place, and the way in which that detail produces the feeling of a place. I'm very interested in the way setting produces feeling in the mind of an observer.

'Titles can sometimes be a problem for me. Some titles, like *Taronga*, I had from the moment I began to write the book. But a title like *Master of the Grove* was one which took days and days and days to come up with. For me the title has to have atmosphere, and has to "home in" on a central idea of the story.'

'I think that every character that I've been able to think of— the good ones and the bad ones—comes from a part of my own personality. This isn't deliberate on my part, but I know that it's happening.

'I don't really use other people that I've observed. Mostly, my characters are made up from thousands of bits of ideas. A face of a stranger in a crowd, a voice heard somewhere. I never write these suggestions down. They just go into the back of my mind somewhere.'

Lloyd Alexander

MADELEINE L'ENGLE

'I have to write through a character I can identify with. Meg, in *A Wrinkle in Time*, is me. I gave Meg brothers because I was an only child and I wanted brothers. I made her good at Maths and bad at English because I was good at English and bad at Maths. But I have all of Meg's faults and flaws and problems. I have the unmanageable hair that I gave her, the nearsighted eyes. I knew just how she felt about herself, because it took me a long time to accept the fact that I would never be small and graceful. I think I made Mrs Murray the kind of mother I'd like to have been with my own children.

'But except for them, my characters are mostly imaginary, although not completely. If you use a real character you are limited by that character, whereas if the character is imaginary it has the freedom to develop and change. My characters are constantly doing or saying things that surprise me. And when that happens, then I know that the writing is going well.

'I like to use imaginary characters, but in settings that I know. This is because the writing of fiction is very sensory. I have to know what a place smells like, what it feels like, and what it sounds like. All of my settings for my stories are places that I've been in. I might exaggerate it—I take a bit out, I make it bigger or smaller, or move it around—but the setting still has to be some place that I'm familiar with with all my five senses.

'The countryside where I live, which became the setting for *A Wrinkle in Time*, is very glacial country. I walk across the great rocks that the ancient glaciers have pushed, and I have a feeling of the earth as being an alive thing. These feelings came into my writing of that book.'

Realistic Fiction and Adventures Stories

SIMON FRENCH

'I put a lot of thought into my characters. I think about what sort of people they are, what sort of place they live in, what they think of their surroundings, and what they think of their lives. I use my characters to tell the story as often as I can. I tend to divide up my stories with plenty of conversation, because that tells the story as well. Conversation gives an extra insight into these characters—how they think, how they view themselves and others.

'Conversation means also that the audience is not faced with page after page of solid description when they read my stories—they can see the characters telling the story as well as the author.

'Some characters are composites of various people— Gabriel in *Hey, Phantom Singlet* is based on about half-a-dozen complete ratbags I went to high school with. Arkie in *All We Know* is based on my two younger sisters, combined with Lisa, a girl I taught during my first year of working in schools. Sometimes characters are not composites but are based on one actual person. Sometimes I invent settings and situations for these characters to operate in, but mostly not.'

LEE HARDING
'I like the characters in my books to evolve and change. I think that a novel is a journey for the reader as well as the characters involved. With only a hazy idea of how the book is going to end, then the characters do have to take over a bit and direct the action, and sort of do the work for you. I try to get away from being the all-powerful writer telling my characters what to do, and instead have the characters have some sort of control over their own lives, within the structure of the book—to have them lead the writer in this strange intuitive way towards the resolution. It's what makes writing, for me, worth doing. If I knew every twist and turn of the plot, it would be boring, which is why I'll never make a lot of money. It's a journey for me to write the book, it's a journey for the characters to pass through it, and a journey for the reader, hopefully.'

ROBERT CORMIER
'As a writer I'm always observing things and looking at people. So my characters are usually composites who seem to spring from the kind of people that I've always been interested in.

'The main character in *The Chocolate War*, however, was based on my son. He was a new student at a school that was in another town, and there really was a chocolate sale that he decided not to take part in. The day he took his unsold chocolates back to school, I watched him walk in with his two bags, and I wondered what he was going to face. I used that old writer's thing: "What if?" That's when I began to write the story.

'In *I Am the Cheese*, the main character there is really myself as a boy, even though I've never written auto-biographically in any of my novels. As I was writing about him, I realised I was writing about my fears as a boy, and about being intimidated by bullies. However, there comes a point in the story when the boy Adam is no longer me. I used those ideas from my own youth, but they weren't enough on their own for a whole novel.

'I'll often introduce a new character in a novel whenever I get into trouble with the writing, and the plot seems to run out of steam. In *I Am the Cheese*, for example, Adam, the protagonist, was having a very drab journey on his bicycle. He was isolated and lonely, his family was withdrawn, and I felt that he needed a little romance and some fun. I thought the reader might need that too, so I introduced the character Amy Hertz, a madcap girl who won my heart over. I wrote on about her relationship with Adam for quite a while, but none of it turned up in the final version. I allow the characters to go on, and sometimes they go wrongly and I have to change them. I don't have to change much, but I have to bring them back to the story. If you get too interested in a character, they tend to run away with you.'

MICHAEL DUGAN

'Although I've pictured characters before I begin writing, changes may occur during the course of writing, as they develop in my imagination.

'I don't "put" anyone I know into a book as a character, although I may combine aspects of different people I know or have met, when I'm building a character.

'And, of course, something of myself often goes in as well.'

CYNTHIA VOIGT

'I have to name my characters before I can start thinking them out and making them similar or different to each other, both physically and mentally. Through naming them, I'm already building up an idea of who they are, what they're going to be, how they're going to react, and what's going to happen to them. Once they have names they become very real to me. I wouldn't be surprised if my characters came to my door and told me that I'd got everything wrong!

'Sometimes the characters come to life before I've placed them in their circumstances. This means that the characters then begin to change where the story is going to.

'I always come to like my characters, even the most unlikeable ones. I never end up despising any of my characters, even if I start out that way, because they're human beings and always have reasons for acting the way that they do.

'Settings for my books can be real places, like the whole coastline in *Homecoming*. Woven into this will be made-up places, like the grandmother's house at the end of Dicey's journey in *Homecoming*. That house came out of my imagination as an expression of everything I love about that part of the United States.

'Sometimes I'll see a place and I'll save the idea of it for a book. Later I'll visualise it, knowing that a character I've thought of would be able to move in that particular landscape. Once, I used the memory of a house I saw in a painting in the National Gallery. I like to draw little maps for myself when I'm writing about a place in a book. I make maps with lollypop trees — I can't draw!'

ROBERT LEESON

'All my characters are originally people that I knew. They're all there in the back of my mind. At night, when

I dream, my head is full of characters who I recognise—people I know from my own family or from school; or people I can't recognise, who I don't seem to have met but probably have. It's just that I've forgotten about them in the front part of my mind, but I remember them with the unconscious part of my mind. So in my dreams, there's a never-ending supply of unusual people. They're people who really exist, that my mind has been working on and changing.

'In my book *Harold and Bella, Jammy and Me*, the "I" character is me. Each of the other characters are two or three people that I knew, all mixed up and put together. Part of the character of Alec in *The Third Class Genie* is me when I was thirteen, because the only way I can know about how people aged twelve or thirteen think and feel is by remembering how I felt myself when I was that age.

'I observe people, but I don't go around with a notebook watching them, because if I did that I wouldn't really get the kind of character I want. I'd get cardboard copies of real people.

'I begin with just a general idea of the characters who are going to be in the story. I may decide that there's going to be six of them, but later on the characters grow in my mind, and as I'm working out the plot I realise that perhaps this character would be better doing that thing, rather than the other character.

'I think a lot about who's going to do what, and I may change it around. It's amazing how it livens up a story if I can change my ideas about which person, for example, is going to be the leader at any particular moment.

'If you can imagine it, the characters in the beginning are like a picture out of focus. The people are just a blurred outline. Then working out the plot is like the lens is being adjusted. The characters come in closer and closer until I can see them in detail, and then eventually I can hear them talking. I always think when I'm plotting a story, that when I see the characters in my mind's eye moving about and talking to each other, and I can hear their voices, then I'm ready to start writing.'

ALLAN BAILLIE

'Between the first draft, the second draft, and the third draft, the characters begin to take shape. The first draft I wrote of *Adrift*, I wrote under the title "The Pirate's Last Voyage". This gave me the idea of a boy, but I didn't know much about him. But as I was writing about him, I was getting a little bit of a glimmer as to what sort of person he was. He was doing certain things. I'd ask myself why he was doing them. Why was he picking on his sister? Why was he trying to pretend to be different people?

'A great deal of all my characters have a little bit of me in them. I don't deliberately try to do this, but even if I write a villain, it has to be a villain from my point of view. I say: "Well, if I was a villain, I'd do this. I'd think that." This is really, of course, Baillie "doing this" or "thinking that".

'Apart from that I do use real characters. For example Vithy, from *Little Brother*, is a real person. I met him on the Cambodian border. I took a few years off him and gave him an elder brother (when in fact he has a younger brother), and a background which I gave him to make him understandable to the reader.

'In the book *Eagle Island*, I knew that I wanted a character who was deaf, and very very independent. A great deal of that character comes from two deaf boys and their parents who I met while writing the story.'

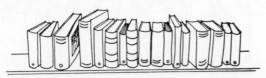

Historical Fiction

ROSEMARY SUTCLIFF

'Usually the place and period that I want to write about comes first, and then the characters step out from that. I wonder about what might happen to the characters, what kind of families they'd have had, what kind of background. And the characters become real people quite quickly.

'The characters grow and change as I write. When I start off I've just written down colour of hair, colour of eyes, likes and dislikes, family backgrounds, and so on. As I go on writing I get to know them as real people, and if I make them do something that is out of character, I think instantly: "No, they wouldn't do that. They wouldn't react in that way."

'Sometimes I feel like I almost become one of the characters, and I develop a very strong empathy with them. Certainly, quite a few of my characters come from within me or from my needs and feelings at the time that I write the book. They're not me, but sometimes they're what I think I'd like to be.

'I use people that I know and observe for my characters, but very seldom the whole person. I nearly always use only bits of them, such as their habits or peculiar tendencies. I'm not really conscious of doing this.'

THE FIRST DRAFT

Very few writers can write a story straight through without needing to change it, despite all their thinking and planning before they start. Many writers go through several drafts, changing and improving their story each time they rewrite. Each writer also approaches the first draft in a different way. While one writer might write it all down quickly to capture the essence of their story, another might carefully polish each sentence before going on to the next. In this chapter, the writers describe how they put their stories together.

Picture Books

MICHAEL FOREMAN
'I start working from my little plan of thirty-two pages. One of the first things I've decided is where my story will take place, so I know that I've got sketchbooks full of drawings. With all the visual material I need at hand, the question becomes one of seeing what will work and where it goes. I work out my pictures first and then I think about the text.

'Usually when I start writing, I find that I'm attempting to do too much for the thirty-two page span, and I edit as I go along by rethinking the pictures and reshaping the text. There are usually more words than I need, too, and quite often the whole thing comes to a complete halt after I've been working on it for a few days, or maybe two or three weeks. Then I work on something else for a while.

'When I go back to it, I try to get rid of a few words. I also try to aim for a visual pattern of words through the book. Sometimes I get a great clump of words in one passage, and then very few words on some other pages. So I rethink the pictures in order to space the words rather better through the book.

'From that stage I then do a full-scale dummy. I decide on the size of the book, and the size of the page—whether it should be upright or landscape. And then I start drawing straight on to that dummy, and at the same time write the text on the pages.

'I rewrite and redraw as I go along, before I show it to a publisher and they make their comments. They don't see it until I'm pretty satisfied with the dummy. I've written a couple of books where the work has gone through that stage, and then I've changed my mind. I've decided that I didn't like it or the way that it was written. I might change my drawing technique and start again.'

STEVEN KELLOGG

'As I work on the story and illustrations, I sometimes become so obsessed with a certain part of the story that I'll work and work on that part. Usually it's a beginning or an ending that I work over and over.

'However, I always try to keep a picture of the whole book going as I work. Often at first the pictures might be very weak, while the text is strong. So I have to bring up the pictures so that the two become locked together in a complete kind of way. It's very important that the text doesn't crowd the pictures and try to do things that the pictures can do better. The words can do something very well, the pictures can do something very well, and together they can tell the story brilliantly if I can let each speak in its own particular way.

'Sometimes the story grows as if to a plan. As I'm working along, if I think of something a little further down the road that I think would be good, then I'll jump ahead and write that down so that when I come to the point when I think that it would work the best, then it's still there waiting for me.

'When I work on the illustrations, I work on a piece of paper which is the same size as the book page. I want the illustration to fit snugly and rightly on the page. I want to feel exactly what way the page is going to feel.

'My preliminary sketches are deliberately unformed, with no carefully drawn expressions or movements, because I want to save a real sense of discovery for the original illustration that I draw after my first draft. This is the one which will appear in the finished book, and hopefully it will appear fresh and alive.

'When I'm going to do the finished illustration, I work from my preliminary sketches. They tell me where I've decided to sit the illustrations in the story, but they leave me enough room to develop the illustration as I draw. That, in turn, can develop the story further, and so I keep working until I decide that it doesn't need shape any more — it fits right into place.

'The amount of time this takes can be very different. Some stories will come together in a couple of months. Some I've worked on for many years.'

ARNOLD LOBEL

'I write in longhand because I don't know how to type, and besides, it would be rather silly to use a typewriter or word processor for the text in a picture book which is fairly small and containable. I do several drafts of the text, because each one becomes messy with all the changes I make. There's constant rewriting, and each page of text probably has as many words crossed out as there are left in.

'As I write each draft I read my manuscript aloud to myself, over and over again. I do this to try and get rhythm and music into my words, and because I know that children's books are read aloud in most cases. I also do it to try and stand back from my story, so that I can hear how it might sound to someone else.

'I do the same thing with my drawings, except that I use mirrors. I hold my drawings up to the mirror so that I can see it in a different way. Another trick I use is to get up in the morning and kind of sneak up on my work, and look at it quickly as though I were a stranger.

'I write my story to a stage where I think it's complete and polished enough, even though I know that the editor is going to help me polish it even further. Then I go ahead with the pictures and I make very complete dummies.

'I paste the text down with the pictures, and my sketches are very finished. Even if something happened to me, the editor could publish the sketches instead of finished artwork, because they are so complete. I do this because I like to see what's going to happen. I want to see how the words work with the picture. Where you turn the page, what kind of picture, what size of picture goes with what amount of text are all very important in a picture book. I work that out very carefully.

'Because my outline sketches are so complete, my finished drawings sometimes lose their freshness. There are many times when I've looked at a finished drawing, and then gone back to look at the preliminary sketch and realised that the sketch was better than my finished work.'

Humour

THOMAS ROCKWELL

'To show you a little bit about how I write a book, I've copied a page of the manuscript of chapter 32 of *How to Eat Fried Worms*. [See page 90.] I have already written the whole first draft straight through, as far as possible, and then I've gone back. So this is the second draft, with the revisions of the third draft on top.

'In the first draft of the last few chapters of the book I wandered off on a twenty-five page tangent trying to find a way to end the book. At the time I didn't realise why I'd gone wrong, I just sensed something was off. All of a sudden I was wandering around in the Great Dismal Swamp. I kept trying to write my way out of it, going on and on with a long involved account of how the boys settled the bet and then planned an elaborate scheme to get the money to pay off the bet. Finally I realised that the essential interest of the book lay in the question: "Who's going to win the bet?" The book should answer that question and then end.

'So I discarded the twenty-five pages and set out to write a new ending. First I had to work out the larger events. How, for instance, could I make the eating of the fourteenth worm entertaining? I'd already done thirteen worms. What could I think up that would be different and amusing? Finally I hit upon the device of a letter: Just as Billy, the boy who's eating the worms, is about to take the first bite of a peanut-butter-and-worm sandwich, a letter arrives, supposedly from a doctor — worms are poisonous, Billy must stop eating them immediately. I wanted to show Billy frightened that he's poisoned himself and then learning that the letter is a fake concocted by the boys who'd bet against him. I decided the quickest way to enlighten Billy would be through his parents. His mother would read the letter, realise it was a fake, and question Billy's sister (who'd brought in the letter). Meanwhile his father . . .

XXXII   Croak

His hand trembling, Billy laid

~~Billy closed his mouth and put~~ the peanut-butter-and-fried-worm
sandwich down on the plate.

~~"Wow," whispered Tom.~~

~~"Emily," said Billy's mother.~~

~~"Emily," called Billy's mother, turning~~

"Mom," do you think . . . ."

"Wow," whispered Tom.

~~Billy's mother gazed thoughtfully at the letter and then turned
and called, "Emily."~~

The screen door banged. Billy's father came into the kitchen,
his ~~jacket over one arm,~~ tie loosened, his jacket over one arm. He
laid his briefcase on the table.

"My God, but "it's hot," he ~~said, glancing around~~ said cheerfully.

Billy staggered to the sink and feebly drew himself a glass
~~of water, slopping it on his~~ of water.

~~"Emily," called his mother, "please come into the kitchen."~~

and Emily
Tom watched Billy, awestruck ~~for the first signs.~~

"Say," ~~said Billy's father,~~ "what's the matter?" *asked Billy's fa*

Trying
The water dribbled down Billy's chin ~~as he drank~~ and onto his
~~chest~~ as he drank. His mind swam. Poison? Paralysis? *Extreme wea*

~~"Emily!" called Billy's mother. "Now!"~~

"Tom," said Billy's father, "what's going on?"

Tom turned, ~~remembered his knife, the initials carved in
the table leg, and blushed, putting his hand blushed, sticking
stuck the hand with the knife holding the open knife into his~~
pointed ~~trouser pocket, wincing winced, the having stabbed his thigh,~~
turned
and ~~pointed at the letter Billy's mother was still clutching
in one hand.~~ *letter lying on the table.*

'With this incomplete, rather vague plot-line in mind,
I started to write. In the first ten lines on the manuscript
you can see I'm trying to work out what Billy and Tom
and Billy's mother will do and say, so that the reader
will see the effect of the letter and the first steps leading
to the disclosure that it's a fake. I started with Billy
fearfully putting down his sandwich; added Tom, then
cut Tom and tried the mother. Then decided I had to
show more of Billy's reaction, and so had him start to
ask his mother if she thinks . . . The prospect is so

horrifying he can't say it — his voice trails off. Tom can only whisper, "Wow." (The reader, of course, already understands that the letter is a fake and so doesn't share the boys' shock and fear, but is amused.) Then, with the mother's call for Emily, I began the process which would lead to Billy's enlightenment.

'And so I went on down the page, inventing and arranging speeches and movements by the characters, so that in the next chapter Billy could eat the sandwich, and the plot could gallop on.

'But when I got to the bottom of the page, I realised that it was all too complicated and slow. It would take me two more pages to work my way out of all those complications. So I decided to cut the mother and leave Billy's enlightenment to his father. Then I reduced the little sister to a spectator, using her only as a means of reflecting and thus emphasising Billy's fright — as I'd used Tom in the first few lines.

'So now I had the scene pretty well worked out. It moved the plot along quickly and in a reasonably amusing fashion.

'Now, that part of the process of writing — discovering and working out what I want to say — can't really be separated from the other part, translating it all into words. As you can see, in the fourth line I first wrote: "'Emily,' said Billy's mother." That didn't seem right somehow, so I tried having her *call, turning* — at which point I decided it wasn't the words but the action that was wrong, and so I crossed out both lines and went back to Billy.

'In my revision I also cut most of the last paragraph on the page. I'd thought it would be amusing to have the other boy, Tom, carving his initials in the leg of the kitchen table — and then he realises it's Billy's father who's just walked in, gets flustered, stabs himself, and so on. But when I read it over, it didn't seem particularly funny — it just seemed to slow things down. I also have a distinct memory, though perhaps I shouldn't mention it, that I was by this time very anxious to finish the book and very weary of revising. Should I make the effort to revise the paragraph? So, for good and bad reasons, I just cut it. Though I think that in a later draft I would probably have forced myself to make the effort if I'd decided the paragraph was vital. All in all the book took me about eight months to write, revise, and so on.'

SUE TOWNSEND

'My actual handwriting is not very clear, so when I rewrite I make sure I write in large, clear letters. I'm also very particular about my punctuation, so writing in large block letters makes my punctuation very clear.

'I'm really very careful about that because if I'm writing a comic line, it has to be timed absolutely right. I need that comma, or that semicolon or that full stop because the timing has to look right on the page. Without punctuation the writing is not flowing at all, so I make sure it is very clear for the typist to type from. Then I have to check the typescript very carefully as well.'

BEVERLY CLEARY

'The hardest part of writing is pushing through to the end of the first draft. I don't read each day's work before I start the next day's work. If I stop, and re-read and work over each day's work, it's a temptation to make each chapter a perfect jewel as I go, and by the time I get to the end of the book I might find that what I wrote at the beginning was all wrong. I lose my perspective if I work on the writing too intensively page by page. It's better to push on and complete a first draft, and then do the revising.

'When I've completed my first draft I type it up (badly) and read the whole thing through. Then it becomes apparent to me what's the important part of the story and what isn't so important, and, perhaps, what needs to be built up a little more.

'After that stage, I put the whole thing away for a month, so that I can come back and read it with fresh eyes. Sometimes more changes are needed, and sometimes not. Then I retype it in my bad typing, but making it readable enough for a professional typist.'

MAX DANN

'I usually write the first draft straight through. Each day I might read through a little bit of what I did the day before, very quickly, but I don't worry too much about mistakes that I've made. I just want to get the idea down while it's fresh, and finish it, without worrying too much about grammar or construction. Even if some of it is a bit rough, I just leave it, because I know I'll clean it up the next time. The important thing is to get the whole idea down the first time, without too many pauses.

'In the first draft I'm looking for ideas, and for pacing and that kind of thing. The second draft is filling the story out, and the third draft is trimming it again. So, while the first draft might take me a month to do, the second draft will make me two months.

'My first draft looks like a mess. I don't think anybody else could understand it, it's so messy. And it's very messy for the second draft as well. Often, if I'm writing out of exercise books, I'll have three or four different books, and the draft swaps from page to page, and to and from different exercise books. If I go away from it for too long, it's a nightmare to try and follow where I've been, because I've just forgotten it. So I make sure I don't stop writing for too long.

'I like to write one thing at a time, or maybe two at the most, because otherwise I just lose touch with it. This happens for two reasons. One is that my drafts are confusing to follow, and secondly I might have forgotten about the story.

'I average about three serious drafts for each piece of writing I do, with maybe a quick read over a fourth time.'

Fantasy

VICTOR KELLEHER

'Although my books go through many drafts, the first draft is absolutely crucial. It's a long, testing business. Unless I really believe in that first draft, I can't go on to make it a good book. It might have all kinds of things wrong with it, but I must believe in it. So I have to write it in a state of total preoccupation. I'm fanatical about it while I'm doing it. Afterwards I can relax within it, and do good creative work and rewriting, because I know that I've somehow captured "World" with all its atmospherics, which is very important to me.

'I write my first draft moving from the beginning through to the end in exact order. I can hold all of this in my head. I can rearrange it all before I write anything down. It's just something I'm good at. I have the ability to hold a lot of sequences and a whole lot of ordered things exactly where they should be, in my head. I don't have to write them down on pieces of paper and shuffle them around. I can make quite drastic changes in my head. I rely on this ability very heavily, as a writer. That's why I spend so much time preparing, because I'm getting a lot of sequences in order. However, I might have to redo these sequences many times in the course of writing the book, so the visual conception will change quite a lot—sometimes a great deal indeed.

'Often I'm scared to write some books. When I'm thinking them out, and the structures become clear in my head, certain episodes or events in the book look more scary than others. I recognise that they are very important scenes, and I wonder if I can really do them and make them work. So what I do is take those scenes and pretend that I'm in the middle of the book, and I write them.

'I work quite hard at them. I write them as though everything else in the book leading up to them is already written. I see if I can get them to work. If I can get them to work, then it makes me confident that I can go back and write the whole book. I then take those episodes, and either destroy them or put them away, because I know that when I really get to them, the "World" of the actual book will have changed what I want to do. Although it's a great temptation to use them, it's like trying to shuffle in something from another book, by the time you get there.

'If I can't write those important central episodes or scenes, if I can't make them work, then I don't write the book.

'I try to write every word and sentence as though it's going to stand for the rest of time. Of course it isn't really like that. One of the hard things about writing for me is that I don't really quite know what I mean to say until I've said it. I don't quite know what I mean to write until I've written it. Often when I struggle with a piece of writing it's because I'm not sure what I want to say. And when I get it right, it's because in trying to write it, I've actually found what I wanted to say. It's difficult to get the meanings clear, both in my head and on the page.

'I also have a strong sense of rhythm in my writing. I'll write out a sentence or a paragraph, or sometimes a phrase, and it will be what I wanted to say but I won't like the rhythm of it in my head, so I won't let it stand. I'll write it and rewrite it immediately, and not go on until it's right.

'Although I know that my first draft is going to end up unreadable to anyone else, because it's scrawled over so much, I still tell myself that each word is going to be the final version. It's a fairytale that I tell myself, because of course the words are going to change. But this fairytale works because it stops me from being slapdash. It makes every moment of concentration a red-hot moment of concentration. And sometimes it means that I get something just right the first time, in a way that I couldn't through revising later on.

'Sometimes hundreds of hours of writing go into the first draft. I always write in longhand for the first draft. I don't work straight on to a typewriter because I'm wary of anything that might make my work look better than it is. I have a pact with myself that I won't put anything in any typewritten form until I can get the sequence of words in my head to sound respectable enough. I don't want to make it respectable before it is. I even write on rotten old bits of used computer paper, quite deliberately, to make it look scruffy. I use a fountain pen to write on both sides of the page, and I don't try to write neatly.

'I like to get a first draft which, although it is incredibly untidy, is right. If I can get that horrible-looking mess to sound good in my head, and I know I've got the story, then I type it up.

'Then I work on that typescript. I scrawl all over it and chop bits out of it, until it looks a bit of a mess, and then I type it again. I keep going through this process until I realise that I'm no longer gaining anything by doing it any further. If I'm lucky, I might go through only three drafts. If I'm not, there might be six drafts. These drafts are total revisions; they're not just crossing a word out here or there. And some of this work can be very boring.

'For me, this is where craftsmanship comes into writing. For the writing to be a professional piece of work, the writer had taken his or her talent and polished it through repeatedly crossing out the work and writing again.'

JANE YOLEN

'Although I'm ready to tell the story, I very often don't know how it will end. I think endings of stories should be both surprising and inevitable. Like anything, if you practise writing enough times you get better at it, and I find I'm getting much more wonderful endings now than when I first began writing and would have to spend much more time looking for the endings. However, I know the character, the setting and the problem, so I start to write the story and somehow all the things come right.

'I actually physically write for only an hour a day, but I'm writing my story all the time — when I'm driving the car, or taking a shower; when I first wake up in the morning, or when I am about to fall asleep. I'm thinking about ideas and processing them, and that's all part of the writing.

'I don't really write a whole story as a first draft. Usually, I'll write the first scene and then I'll put it aside and come back to it the next day. I find it difficult to know whether I wrote the scene well enough immediately after having written it. In fact, I rarely even remember it, because I go so quickly through the first part of the story the first time I write it.

'I can't jump in and write the endings or the middles first. I really need to move through time and space the same way that the story moves through time and space. So I start at the beginning and work in the order that the story unfolds.

'The next day, I go back and read it as if I were the reader. That way I try to see what works and what doesn't work. I make changes, and perhaps add a little bit to it, and then the next day I might come back and add some more. I go over it and over it — sometimes as many as fifteen or twenty separate times — and I always read it aloud to myself to see how it sounds. I always think that the first paragraphs in my stories are much more polished than the ending parts, because I go over them more times. Each time I come back and do some more work, I start from the beginning again.

'Sometimes I cross it all out, and sometimes I only change one word. But I always try to get back to it within three or four days, to see what I've done. I'll keep doing this for perhaps a week, and then I may reach a point where there's nothing more in that story. It may sit again for a day, a week, a month, six months, maybe even several years, before I go back to it.

'The time it takes for me to write a book really varies. I wrote one book in three days, and one book in nineteen-and-a-half years. I've taken four or five years to write a very short book, and written much longer books in six or eight months, so it has nothing to do with how big a book is. It has to do with getting the story right, and sometimes it takes many years for me to tell the story that's meant to be told.'

Realistic Fiction and Adventure Stories

ALLAN BAILLIE

'The first draft is sheer drudge, and the first thing I do is work out the ending. For example, the last line in *Little Brother* was written, mentally, before I wrote the first word. So I knew where the story was going to go. This means that in the writing of the book I have to work out when I'm going to let the reader know enough to make sure that they keep reading.

'The first draft is also just shovelling in things. That's when I'm putting things down, when little ideas are going in. I know, now, that the character will take off, or do something, between the second and third draft. It's like the characters turn around and say: "I don't say things like that!" Or: "I don't do that!" And I say "O.K.", and away we go.

'That is, in fact, the greatest fun and the greatest part of writing—being told to do something by the character.

'In the second draft, there's a feeling developing. The characters are changing and interacting with each other, and the book is beginning to almost write itself, in a way.'

LEE HARDING

'I do a lot of drafting and a lot of revision. I work very intensely over the first page, and then I take off and I might get about a third of the way through the projected novel. I go right back to the beginning again, and then I forge right ahead and get to the end usually, this time. With this, I've pretty well got down what I want in the novel.

'Getting out the first draft is a lengthy, painful experience. It's like being a sculptor and starting with a slab of rock, chiselling it away, trying to find a face. I feel like I'm trying to find the story, chiselling it out of nothing. Then I do about two or three drafts after that. The drafts are mostly a process of rendering down, getting it exactly right, rather than addition of further material.

'These other drafts are the fun part. I know where I've been and what I've wanted to say, and I know that I want to shave a bit off this scene, or cut a bit of that dialogue. These later drafts are very exciting because I know I'm getting closer and closer to the final polish. This, for me, is the most exciting part of writing.'

SIMON FRENCH

'Once my stuck together bits of paper are shuffled around into the order I've devised, and typed out, I then go back and insert new portions of description, new conversations perhaps, or completely new scenes. I might cut up those pages again and sticky tape them together in a different order, although sometimes segments of a story remain as I first wrote them. At any rate, I often wind up with chaptered pieces of paper several metres long pegged up next to the desk. I read through them several times over, throwing more sentences in, correcting other sentences, altering descriptions, trying to improve things all the time.

'So, it's an ongoing process of rewriting, revision, and piecing a story together until I'm satisfied with the order of events, the balance, and the quality of description and conversation.

'Once I have a complete idea in my mind of how the people in the story should appear to the reader, and what the story is setting out to tell, what I see on paper should reflect my total knowledge and understanding of the people and situations described. This point of story writing is when the need for revision ceases.

'I read my text to myself over and over. I read it to myself aloud because, having been a teacher and presented stories by other people to kids, I know the sort of text and storyline that read really well and leave the audience wanting for more.

'I really love books where I can reach the end of the story and wish there were more of it. I try and achieve that with my own books.'

ROBERT CORMIER

'There are two things being worked at while I'm writing. There is the concept, and there are the mechanics. The concept is what has to happen; the mechanics are how I'm going to make it happen. The mechanics are easy because that's technical. You can always figure out how to do it. The concept is the important thing.

'I do the direct writing on the typewriter. If I want to capture a scene or an emotion or a character, I go like the wind and don't worry too much about how well it's written. If I have a problem with something, I leave it and go on, and fill the gap later. Then I do an awful lot of rewriting.

'I edit my writing constantly as I work. It bothers me to the point of sometimes holding me up in my writing if I haven't polished the last thing I wrote. I suppose it's like building a house. If I know that the first floor isn't that well done before I start the second floor, then I'm afraid it might collapse. So I polish the syntax, the grammar and the punctuation before I go on.

'I'm very careful with word constructions and punctuation. Very little is accidental. When I want to slow the reader up, the sentences are longer and a little more ponderous than they were before. When I want action and go, the sentences are shorter. My sentences are clear and simple, and I read my work aloud.

'You can't hear me, but I'm mouthing the words all the time. This is a fantastic help because it shows me the awkward sentences which would interrupt the reader. I want the reader to keep reading. So, as I rewrite my work I cut out complicated words, so that people are reading, not running for a dictionary. I try to keep them reading with rhythmical sentences. Sometimes a sentence ends and I sense that it needs another word in there, just to complete a kind of rhythm.'

MICHAEL DUGAN

'To anyone but myself my first drafts would be unreadable, due to my messy handwriting. The first draft of a novel follows the synopsis, and usually contains too much explanation. The second draft cuts out material, tidies and adds colour to characters. Sometimes there will be a third typed draft before I'm happy with the book.

'With picture book manuscripts I usually have some idea of the illustrations in my head, but I don't tell these to the illustrator unless he or she asks me to. I think that illustrators are creative people in their own right, who should interpret the story as they wish.

'However, I did give the illustrator, Jane Burrell, my plans for illustrations to *A House for Wombats*. This was because the text gave no hint as to the pictures, and it would have been almost impossible for her to visualise the illustrations from the story alone.'

'Ideally, because of all my planning, when I finally do start writing a book I write it right the way through on my typewriter, and just correct a few words here and there. I don't like rewriting. Apart from two occasions, every book I've written has been written once only.'

Robert Leeson

CYNTHIA VOIGT

'I usually write on a typewriter, and I always start writing at the first word on page one. I write in order through to the end. But when I know that it's going to go slowly, that I'm trying to discover it, I write with a pencil, in longhand. I might write the first paragraph, and then come back the next day and realise it isn't right, and so rewrite the first two paragraphs. It's a juggling act. I know what I want to say but I also know I have to discover what I have to say.

'Once I know what I want to do I usually go pretty fast, but it takes a number of false starts. I cross out and rip up and write it out to the end, but as the characters say things and do things and tell me more, I have to revise the whole outline because the whole story changes.

'Some things become unnecessary, and other things become possible. An example of this happened when

I was writing *Homecoming*. Originally the book was only half as long. Then, while I was working on the second chapter, a character just leapt up out of the typewriter. It's a dark typewriter, and this character just came out saying things, and it was the grandmother. I could hear her voice. I didn't sit down and think her up. It was just that there was a vacant space and there she was, like Captain Kirk coming out of the Enterprise! So I made the book twice as long, because once she appeared I knew who she was, I knew where I wanted her, and I knew what she could do.

'I think somehow she must have been created by all those outlinings of the first part of the book, so I then had to keep revising my outline, while I was writing.

'The first rough draft is really unreadable. When I get a chapter and I think it's working, I type it up using about one and a half spaces for each line. This is fast typing, complete with errors. I then type a fair copy again, but each time I retype it I'm constantly changing a sentence or a word or a scene, because as I read it it might not seem to work.

'I'm very fast. It takes me about three or four months after I start writing to get what I call the "presentation draft" out, which means that it's ready to be read and to undergo whatever revision is needed.'

Historical Fiction
ROSEMARY SUTCLIFF

'After I've brewed on the shape of my story, and done all the research I've been able to think of, I face that first white blank piece of paper. This happens every day, and it's daunting to try to think how to get the story put down—how to get the right words and the right shape to the sentences. I find if I'm not careful, I'll spend a whole morning just sitting and looking at that paper.

'I always have to say to myself: "Don't worry about

it being the right sentence, just get something down. You can put it right next time. Get something down. It doesn't matter how bad it is."

'I always have to write two or three drafts, so I force myself along like that quite often. I rework my writing a lot, so the first draft is almost unreadable, sometimes even by me.

'The second draft has quite major surgery done to it. I drop off characters that have faded out halfway because there's nothing more for them to do, and introduce other ones that didn't come in early enough before. Then the third draft is a matter of polishing.

'The third draft is a delight, because all the real solid work is done. I just take pleasure in getting the subtle bits, and the colours and the shading. If it's good, then it feels right. It has the right smell. Something deep inside me says that it works. Then a typed copy is sent away to the publisher.'

Poetry

JACK PRELUTSKY
In chapter 4, 'Getting Ready to Write', Jack Prelutsky talked about writing a poem about a boneless chicken. He continues here, and describes the many drafts needed to complete the poem.

'I put all my ideas about eggs and chickens on to the word processor so that they're readable, and as I'm doing this, new ideas will come up and I'll start seeing rhyming pairs and additional information. I then take a printout and sit back in my big reclining chair with it, and a yellow legal pad, and I start writing on the printout, adding things on the pad. Then I go back to the word processor.

'This can happen in ten minutes, or it can happen in six months. It goes back and forth, and some poems come out very quickly. Some I go back to and back to, and do dozens of rewrites.

'I've now finally decided what kind of an egg the boneless chicken is going to lay. Boneless chickens lay scrambled eggs. Now it's just a matter of arranging the poem and building to a conclusion. I need a mood—a proper voice for the poem. To start by writing

"Once there was a boneless chicken . . ."

seems a little flat. I decide that I need to let the chicken do the talking, because a boneless chicken would have an interesting point of view. I give the chicken a puzzled voice, as if it doesn't understand why it isn't treated the way other chicken are treated. Yet it's very proud of itself. It's proud to be boneless. Boneless is beautiful!

"I have feathers fine and fluffy.
I have lovely little wings.
But I lack superstructure
to support these splendid things."

After many tries, this is the voice I keep for the poem.'

EVE MERRIAM

'I do a draft of the poem in pencil, or in my favourite coloured ink, which is purple. I write on lots of yellow, lined legal pads, and the papers just mount in the wastepaper basket as I do them over and over again.

'Then I'll transfer to the typewriter. I'm a terrible typist—I use just one finger on each hand on a manual typewriter. I make more corrections and rewrites there.

'When I look at my drafts I'll have corrections at the top, or in the middle or the bottom, and it's a real puzzle to work it out.

'As I rework the poems I feel a bit like a dentist picking around doing the fine work. The language of the poem has to be beautiful, and if I get too many consonants together, or too many sibilants together, then there's something that's not beautiful about it.

'So I'll do that sort of thing only on purpose. For example, I wrote a poem which was meant to be read out loud, and I wanted it full of sibilants. It was called "The Serpent", and I purposely chose words that would have a lot of sinuous qualities.

'Otherwise, I try to avoid too many "s"s in a row. I try to avoid words that will end in "ed" when the next word begins with a consonant, because of the "tt" sound that results.

'I read all the poems aloud to myself, over and over. It's important to read any poem several times, because the first time gives a sense of the music; the second time gives the meaning.

'As I redraft the poems over and over again, I'm looking at how it sounds, the look of the letters and words on the page, and the look of the lines on the page. However, I can only juggle just so much. So the two things that I have to do simultaneously are to have a sense of what I'm saying, and a sense of the musicality of it.

'So I start, and it may be crude and there may not be much music in it. I know I have to change a phrase, but I don't want to lose the sense of the poem. So I try to make it more musical. Or sometimes I might be so infatuated with the music of it that the sense is not coming across. It's difficult to keep juggling these two things, but it's thrilling.'

Non-Fiction

SEYMOUR SIMON

'I find that once I have my rough outline, and I've done enough research so that I know what I'm going to do, it's far better for me to start writing. Then what I want to know and find out more about becomes clear as I'm writing it.

'I always go from step one to step two, and I always write by going from the very simple ideas to the more complicated ones. I try to give lots of examples, and I try to write as if I'm talking to a friend. I always read aloud what I write or, if I don't, I hear the sentences in my head as I'm writing. I try to write as I talk. And when I read it aloud, if it doesn't sound right to me, I'll rewrite it until it does. So I'm very aware of how things sound, and I also try to write so that if I were reading it, it would be very clear to me.

'As I write the words I rewrite immediately, so that by the time I finish with a chapter it's close to the way it's going to come out. I enjoy that enormously, because I like playing with words. I like tuning my words, so I edit my own writing word by word as I go. I like to make the sentences flow as effortlessly and simply as possible. I rarely do a major rewrite.'

WHEN THE WRITING ISN'T GOING WELL

All authors face that awful moment when they realise that something just isn't working. Even so, few of them discard their work as a complete failure. Instead, they try to see what can be used. Here the writers discuss the problems that often cause their writing to falter, and describe the techniques they use to overcome their difficulties.

Picture Books

STEVEN KELLOGG

'I always have problems with each book as I'm writing it, and I think that this is healthy. It forces me to work harder, to think harder—to think more deeply into my thoughts or my feelings or my experiences, or wherever the story is coming from, and find the real truth that I think is right for that book. If I try to create the book too quickly or too easily, I don't think that the book really has a chance to reflect my best efforts.

'I can tell that the book isn't working when the story or the pictures lose pace. The story starts to become heavy, and the words and pictures come more and more slowly. I can't think of the words, or the words and pictures don't tell the events and the feelings the way that I want the reader to see them.

'If that happens, and I can't work my way through it on the spot, then I stop and do something else. Usually I do something totally away from writing a book. It means it's time to get some exercise—to go outside, to go in the woods, or walk down the street.

'Often no one else can help me. It just takes time and effort. One story which I wrote had problems with the ending. I worked on it, put it away, and then worked on it some more, and kept doing this over nearly fifteen years. Suddenly it just came together last winter. Either I'd changed and grown enough, or I was just working in the right time and place, but I was able to write and draw my way through all the problems and the whole story came together.

'It also takes time and effort to discover when the writing and illustrations are finished. I think that when I was first writing books, I had to overwrite and over-draw in order to learn when I'd pushed too far. Gradually I've developed a certain instinct and can let the work speak to me and say: "You've finished. Don't touch me again. I'm just right."'

Humour

BEVERLY CLEARY

'I don't believe that "writers' block" exists, but there are times when I bog down and I know I need to do something different for a while. I think that not being able to write comes from pressuring yourself too much, so I break the pressure for a while by doing something with my hands—making something. The story is still always going on in the back of my mind.

'Because I don't structure my stories before I begin writing, I just pray that they're going to happen. The stories happen or they don't. I've torn up two almost-completed books because the story wasn't happening and there was nothing I could do about it. I threw them away and started on another book. I don't return to them, although parts of what I'd put in those books may return up in other books. Their original ideas I won't use again.

'When the writing isn't working, it's like walking over a carpet that's got a golf ball underneath it. You just feel that it's there. It might be just one or two words too many, and I'll whisk them out. I rewrite my work at least twice, and sometimes, with the plays, I rewrite them seven or eight times.'

Sue Townsend

MAX DANN
'When I can't get any ideas, or nothing is happening, I always push on anyway. It means, nevertheless, that I might write for two days or two weeks and hate everything I do. But I know I have to push myself to go on, because eventually it's going to break and I'll be happy with what I'm writing. I then throw away the rubbish I was writing in that two weeks, because it wasn't what I was after—it was just a way in which I came to the writing and the ideas that I really wanted to reach.

'I'd never just sit in a room all day and do nothing. I'd rather write, even if I know that what I'm writing is worthless. It's more productive than doing nothing, and one thing will lead to another. I find I have to do that to come up with the idea.

'I've occasionally thrown away something that I've written because I know it just hasn't worked, but I usually try to salvage something from it.

'I've written manuscripts which nobody wanted, and that's a bit disappointing, but I have to accept that. I don't throw those stories away. I've kept everything I've written since I was sixteen. Often I can't use anything from them, but they're all an important part of learning how to write. A manuscript will come back from a publisher, perhaps with an explanation as to why the publisher doesn't want it, and that can help you stand back and see what's wrong with it. But if I don't agree with what the publisher says, then I keep on sending the manuscript off until someone does want it. You've got to trust yourself.

'But sometimes I know, afterwards, that it wasn't good enough, and I just file it away.'

Fantasy

VICTOR KELLEHER

'I've sometimes worked out a structure and during the writing process that structure has failed. I've taken the wrong idea and it just hasn't worked for me. That's a painful process, because I'm the kind of writer who, at different points in writing a book, feels that what I'm writing is garbage. Sometimes that goes on for some time, and I work on in the dark, just hoping that things will get better.

'I now know, through experience, that I'm going to hit those walls repeatedly, and that I've just got to stick with it. The real question is: "Have I just lost my confidence again, or has the central idea really failed to work out? Is what I'm writing really terrible?"

'I'm not a writer who works with a high level of confidence. If I did, I think I'd write worse. If you have too little confidence, I think you become a bad writer. If you have too much confidence you cannot be critical of your own work, and you become a bad writer.

'So, every now and then, I reach a point where I say: "Not only do I think this is garbage, it really is garbage."

And I throw it in the bin. I don't hold on to it for several years, because if I were to come back to it some years later I'd have changed too much. It would be like two different writers working on it. But I do sometimes rescue an idea, or hold on to a memory of material and find that it re-emerges in a later book.

'Writing is a very lonely occupation, and it isn't easy to make all the decisions by myself. When the writing isn't working I just keep trying. I just keep blasting away. If I find that I'm sailing round in circles, I've got to stop the boat. I've got to find which way I'm going. Sometimes I walk up and down the room for days, in order to dredge up a sort of little conscience figure from the back of my mind which is saying: "Look! You know this isn't going anywhere. Face up to the facts. Scrap this and start again here and take this direction . . ."

'This is easily said, but finding it out can be a painful process. You can't get any help from anyone else, because they can't be inside your own dream or vision or story.'

LLOYD ALEXANDER

'I have rewritten a whole novel three times from beginning to end—every page, three times. I didn't just alter a word or the punctuation. It was a disastrous, terrible thing to do.

'Generally, my own judgement tells me that it's not working. I try to convince myself that it's fine. I tell myself that it will look better tomorrow. And I think that maybe just a little fixing will do the trick. But sometimes I know in my heart, secretly, that the writing is bad, and at some point I've got to face up to the truth.

'Often, it's because the story has started to move itself away from my original synopsis. What seemed like such a marvellous idea eight months before seems terrible now. This isn't a bad thing, because it means that I've changed, developed and grown in some way. It just means that despite my moans and sniffles, I realise that I have to start again. I have to rethink the whole thing. I can say to myself: "Yes, I'm right in keeping this, but I'm wrong if I keep that." I'll throw it out.

'But sometimes, part way through a novel I have to discard the whole thing, because the problem may not be the page that I'm working on. When I have serious difficulties, it's usually because I did something wrong a long way before, which is now just beginning to show. It's like a time bomb.'

JANE YOLEN

'I find out that a story isn't working or isn't good enough in two ways. I might send it to my publishers and get many rejection letters, all of which say the same thing, so the weakness must be there. The other way comes from my own self-filtering system. It's important to be critical of my own work. I then keep working away each day at the story, or I put it aside and come back to it a long time later with a new way of looking at it.

'I never throw anything out. Sometimes a piece of writing that I think is disgusting and horrible and awful might (a day or a week or a year from now) seem different, because I will be different. I can look at the writing differently later on and perhaps see how to change it.

'The book that took nineteen-and-a-half years to write, I wrote five totally separate ways. It was a short novel for teenagers, and I had a terrible time chipping away until I found the story I wanted to tell. In the first drafts of the story I killed off the mother; I tried it with the father dead; I wrote it as complete fantasy; I wrote it as part-fantasy; then I wrote it as totally realistic. Each time I was telling a slightly different story, but it wasn't until the very last time that I found the story that I wanted to tell.

'It used to bother me that when I put my story down

on paper it always fails. It's never the story that's in my head. I keep reminding myself that the story I've written down has its own beauty, and that it may be the one story which really touches someone and be important to them.'

Realistic Fiction and Adventure Stories

ALLAN BAILLIE

'There's a struggle to put everything together so that the book will arrive at the ending I've already worked out, but I don't force it to unfold in certain ways. I readjust events or characters to fit in with the direction of the story. If I try to force a character to do something that he or she wouldn't, then it doesn't work. I can see it. I suppose it's experience which allows me to read a line and know that it isn't right. And if you live with and write about your characters for a long time, you do know when you've dropped a clanger!

'I've had four book manuscripts rejected. One book almost didn't get printed. It was the ninth publisher who finally accepted it. I have rewritten manuscripts in an effort to get them accepted.

'It feels very miserable when a publisher returns a manuscript saying that they don't understand it, or they don't want it. It feels like you've spent a year or a year and a half for nothing.

'I've also written almost a whole book and decided for myself that it wasn't going to work. It's hard to decide this, but I've got to get away from my ego and realise that no one is probably going to want to read it. Also, I realised that I was pushing hard to try and write it. In all successful books, the pushing gets easier somewhere in the first draft—it begins to take off. In this one, I was just plodding away. It just wasn't moving.

'I don't throw it away. I keep it, and it just quietly mildews in my office. I don't think that I'd try to write it again, but there are parts of it which I could use somewhere else.'

ROBERT CORMIER

'I've often finished a novel and gone over it and started again from page one. I have boxes of rewritten pages. I don't mind this because I think it's an advantage. A brain surgeon has to get it right the first time, but a writer can always rewrite and fix and tinker and get a better word. That's the beauty of language. You can always seek a better way of saying something.

'I write better on different days, too. Sometimes I might only be at my typewriter for an hour and a half, but the words are really dancing and singing on the page. Other times I can sit there for six or seven hours, and the words are plodding and don't seem to come and they won't move the right way. The answer is to just keep doing it day after day.

'I started a novel a while ago, and worked very hard and long on it. I worked every day for a couple of months, and then finally decided that it was going no place. I was experimenting with something new and it just wasn't working. So I put it aside and began another one the next day.

'I have two novels on my shelf right now which haven't sold. I've had my share of rejection slips, but I'm not upset by that because I enjoyed writing them.

'If the plot seems to have run out of steam, or I've gone as far as I can and yet I know I've got to get the story shifted to somewhere else, I might introduce a new character. Sometimes, what I'm writing is going in the wrong direction. For example, I thought a character I wrote about was very interesting, and yet I had a sense that she wasn't very likeable. The reader wouldn't like her. The novel was really finished when this happened and I hadn't been able to control it. The problem was solved for me by an editor who suggested that the character should always be seen through her boyfriend's eyes. That softened the picture of her, but it meant that I went back and changed the whole book. It meant that I had about five or six good chapters written about her that I simply didn't use.'

CYNTHIA VOIGHT

'As I re-read my work I make notes on the side about what doesn't seem to be working. Sometimes it's the story going false or the character going false. Sometimes I'm pushing what I want to have happen. Sometimes it's my style of writing. And sometimes it's the way I'm reading my writing that particular day. I have to be careful that I'm not undermining my own work.

'I get a feeling about the story. The idea might be muzzy and the focus not clear, because I'm discovering the story as I go along. This isn't a matter of what happens, or who says what, but it comes from *how* I write what I write, and *how* what happens happens. I have to work out whether it isn't working because I haven't worked on it long enough, or I haven't thought it out thoroughly enough.

'If there's something I don't like about a book that I've written, I put it aside for a couple of months and do something else. I then come back to the work and go through it again, looking for the focus I want and trying to get it right. I like the book to go away and get read at this point, by my family or editor, even though I know I'm not through with it. It helps me to know what to do with it.

'I don't throw away what doesn't work, but I tend to forget about where it is. It's the present process of writing that I like, and I don't really go back to rewrite work that wasn't successful. I still have manuscripts rejected, and that's painful. But once something is accepted and published, being rejected is never quite so painful again.

'I never have moments when I have no ideas for another story, but I do have moments when what I want to write doesn't seem to want to be written! And sometimes I do need to shift pace and to try and write using other patterns, because sometimes I'm not thinking.'

ROBERT LEESON

'Very often, when I find my story as I've worked it out is dull and uninteresting, I swap the characters around. I think a lot about who's going to do what, and change it around, and it's amazing how it can liven a story up. I get the character you'd least expect to suddenly take the lead, and the whole story changes and becomes more interesting.

'Most people run into trouble because they try to write a book in the way that they read it. When you read a book it's like going on a long walk. You set off and you follow the path, and what you don't realise is that the writer has prepared a whole map. The writer knows where the forests and towns are, where the mountains and rivers and everything else in that landscape are, before they show you where the path is that you're going to follow. There are lots of things the writer knows about that landscape, that the writer isn't even going to write down in the story. So the difference between writing and reading is the difference between making a map, which is what the writer does, and going on a journey, which is what the reader does. This means that it's the work you do before you start writing that is important.'

MICHAEL DUGAN

'During my early teens, when I first started trying to write a book, my main difficulty was that I was always starting books but lacked the stamina to finish them. I must have written ten chapter ones, fewer chapter twos, and faded out with two chapter threes. I hadn't learnt that I needed to plan a book before I began writing.

'Sometimes, if a story isn't right, it helps to leave that story for a while and work on something else. I wrote *Melissa's Ghost* over four months, and then had to put it aside for nearly eighteen months, because I couldn't see why the story didn't work. When I went back to it, I saw that I'd departed from the main story at one stage and had introduced unnecessary characters.

'On two occasions, I've rewritten an entire book.'

Poetry

JACK PRELUTSKY

'It happens all the time. After I've written a poem and then gone back later to read it again, then I can see the poem hasn't worked.

'I can tell this because I don't enjoy it. If I don't enjoy reading it, no one else is going to enjoy reading it. If it doesn't sound right, if it's flat, I know I should take the idea and do something more with it.

'I'm getting better at doing that, probably just through practice. I learnt by doing, by writing and polishing what talent I might have had to start with.

'There is help along the way. I read a lot, and I've never met any good writer who doesn't read. I read lots of other poetry and I've got many ideas from the work of other poets. I also listen to my wife and to my editor, because sometimes I'm so close to the work I don't have a clear picture of what I'm doing. I think something is right, and it could be completely wrong.'

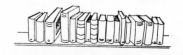

EVE MERRIAM

'I go through stages as I write each poem. The first stage is elation at the idea and how the poem is going to work. Then comes the feeling that what I've written is awful. How could anyone write anything as dopey as this! And then I come to some sort of middle ground where I think that it's not the best poem in the world, but it's not the worst.

'So I then try to cool off about it. I try not to look at it for a couple of weeks. Then I go back and sneak a look at it and see that perhaps this part works. This could be better. This may be a bit confused and not clear.

'Then I finally get to the point where I have to realise that this is the most that I'm capable of doing with it now. The poem is as good as I can do, and I have to let it go out into the world. I have to realise that I can never achieve perfection.

'I do get my poems rejected sometimes. Then it is very important to know that my work is my work, and not everyone will appreciate it or want to publish it. I try not to let myself be discouraged and I don't give up.

'What I try to do when my poems are rejected is first of all not fall apart. Then I sort of gather my courage and I look at my work carefully. If I've received criticism, then I check out that criticism to see if my poems do have weaknesses that I haven't been able to see. Or I may decide that it wasn't the right magazine or editor for my kind of poetry, and the poetry may be right for something else.'

Non-Fiction

SEYMOUR SIMON

'Sometimes, because I've been working very hard on a book, I develop a sort of blindness about what I'm writing. It no longer makes sense to me and I have no idea if it's any good or not. When that happens, I have to go on to a different part of the book, or even a different book completely. I have to step back for a while and let it sit. It's very important, though, not to let a very long time pass between one writing session and another, because it becomes too hard to start again.

'I also sometimes lose enthusiasm for what I'm writing about three-quarters of the way through, because I'm already thinking about my next project. I just try to finish the book as best I can.'

REVISION AND THE
ROLE OF THE EDITOR

Picture Books

STEVEN KELLOGG

'I constantly rewrite my books. This means that I change and correct what I've written, usually to try and make the story more concise, and to make the story and pictures work more smoothly together. I rewrite so that the text and the pictures tell their part of the story in their own way. I want the text and the pictures to dance in response to each other, because this is what makes the picture book special. It's something for the eye and something for the ear.

'Sometimes a good editor can be very helpful, especially if I'm stuck and can't go on writing. It needs to be someone who cares about the story, and cares about the way it turns out; who will read it and give me some sense of direction, so that I can work myself around whatever is the problem.

'The book that I'm working on can also become so important to me, and so much a part of me, that I forget about how other people are going to see the work, and an editor can help me there. I may not like to hear that the writing is bogged down and that it isn't communicating well, but I have to be able to trust that criticism

121

from the editor and go back and work on the writing again.

'I also need to be my own editor, my own critic, my own judge of how the book is going.'

ARNOLD LOBEL

'I have always valued criticism and help from my editors. I've never finished a book without doubting whether it was trash or treasure.

'No matter how many times I rewrite it, I still make mistakes. I have done some very odd things—like writing a story about a particular character and then suddenly switching the viewpoint to another, less important, character. I'll re-read what I've written a hundred times and not notice that I've done something like that, because I have blind spots about my own writing. But my editor will pick it up instantly.

'When my editor doesn't like what I've done, I put it away and work on something else. Then six months later I'll look at it again, to see if the editor was right. Often by then I can see that the editor was, and I'll rewrite the parts that don't work. Mostly the story is then better than it was originally, which is why I rely very much on my editor.'

Humour

BEVERLY CLEARY

'When I revise my first drafts I look for and change certain things. I look for words that are repeated, or scenes that can be condensed and shortened. Once in a while, characters wander in for no particular reason and I have to shoo them out.

'And then I ask myself: "What's the most important part of the story?" And: "Have I done all that I can, to that part?"

'I learnt to ask myself these two questions from my

first editor. She told me that beginning writers often get so carried away with their stories that they zoom right past the most important part of the story which might be in their minds but they don't get it down on paper.

'My family reads my books after I have finished them and before they go to the publisher. If I've used any of my own children's personal experiences, I ask them if they object to me writing that part. When I wrote *Mitch and Amy*, my son, who actually was Mitch in the book, pointed out that it was impossible to ride a bicycle with a banana in your hip pocket! I saw his point and changed it.

'But you have to write to please yourself. Once you start trying to please other people, then originality is lost. Except for the two questions my first editor taught me to ask myself, I find it a pretty good idea to ignore advice.'

MAX DANN

'I never get anyone to read my drafts, until the book is finished. I used to get anybody who was passing to read my writing when I first started writing. But I found that while it was helpful in one way, it was also fairly destructive in another way, because most people don't know what they're talking about.

'For people who are starting off writing, and for most writers, one thing they really need is a dependable critic, someone they really trust—like a good editor. That's really important.

'Different editors do different things. They help me with ideas. I couldn't do it without an editor. For example, even though I'd finished my third or final draft, there'd always be problems with it. The editors would often be able to recognise weak areas, which usually I know about as well but have been trying to ignore!

'I don't always do what the editors suggest, unless I

think they're right. It's always a bargain with editors. You have to give a little, and get a little.'

Fantasy

VICTOR KELLEHER

'A good editor can look at your work with sympathy, but at the same time with a critical, beady eye. They can enter into your world and yet keep one foot out of it, enough to be able to say: "Hey! What are you doing here?" They can cast new and different beams of light on to your work, and highlight things that you haven't really thought of.

'But if an editor suggests a change in your work that you feel in your bones is wrong, you've got to be able to say "no". However, there's no harm in making "compromise" changes which meet an editor half-way without damaging your conception, if he or she is really worried about something.

'Sometimes an editor can be totally right.'

JANE YOLEN

'I do get other people to read my work before I send it to a publisher. My husband reads everything and he's very helpful. I also meet every week with a group of five professional writers, and we read what we're working on aloud to one another and have it criticised. I also send it off to my agent, and she tells me what she thinks of it. So, five or six people read my work before it goes off to an editor. It's usually just about complete before I let anyone read it. I don't show it to anyone halfway through.

'Sometimes their criticisms cause me to change what I've written. I listen to what they say because they may be right or they may be wrong. I think about it, and I may totally reject it or I may decide to accept it. After all, it's my name which is going to be on the book.'

Realistic Fiction and Adventure Stories

SIMON FRENCH

'*Hey, Phantom Singlet* was written when I was mainly twelve and thirteen, and was read progressively by the kids in my class at school, who were the people I was writing about at the time. That was very helpful to me in most ways, but I did wind up with a book that was very cluttered—too much happening and too many characters. There were also things suggested for inclusion by the kids at school that I wish had never been included, because utlimately they didn't really belong in the plot. But it was, overall, a helpful process for me, because I was able to really tune in to my audience, who were the same age as me at the time. I'd also set out to write for myself an Australian book with a suburban Australian setting, because most of the books in the library at school were either English or American.

'*Cannily Cannily* wasn't read in full by anyone else, until it was typed up in its initial form and ready to send to the publisher. At this stage, I had one of the children on whom I'd based Trevor in the story read it.

'These days I feel happier working by myself, and pushing myself to improve my writing, before I show anything to anyone. When the book is at a fairly complete typed stage, I'm then content to have family and friends read it and provide me with feedback and corrections. I can then go back and, for the final published draft, include such corrections and last minute fine tuning.

'With *Cannily Cannily* I had a friend experienced in coaching football, and he helped me add the necessary realism to the football aspects of the story, because I hadn't played sport as a child. What I'd written was what

I'd seen from a distance as a spectator-spy at childrens' football matches when researching the initial plot for myself.

'The editors at publishing companies I've come into contact with are another source of assistance. *Hey, Phantom Singlet* was initially rejected by several editors, who suggested that my characters lacked depth and various situations in the storyline lacked description. Even though the final product seemed to still have a cast of dozens, I did act on those initial suggestions from editors, and the book was rewritten several times over.

'With *All We Know*, my editor suggested cutting out portions of events and description. I was happy for that to happen, because the story is introspective rather than action-packed and there was a need to heighten its appeal and immediacy.'

ALLAN BAILLIE

'After I first wrote *Adrift*, when it was still called "The Pirate's Last Voyage", an editor read the manuscript and decided that it was too short. She suggested that I could do one of two things: I could either write another thirty pages of further incidents; or give a little bit more background to the boy, to suggest some idea as to why he was behaving the way he was. We both thought this was the best idea. So I went back and started rewriting, and as I did, the character of the boy became more solid.

' A publisher's reader suggested that I ought to have a small mystery running through the beginning and most of the chapters of *Little Brother*, to keep puzzling the readers. So I put in the mystery of the brother talking about the "lines". I used my computer and simply fitted the sentences in all through the chapters, using cut-and-paste.

'I do show my first draft to people such as my wife

and children. *Megan's Star* was my first attempt at having a heroine, and I needed someone of the opposite sex to give me some feedback. I always consider what people have to suggest.

'I show my writing to my editors when I think I've got it right. I'll have done two complete drafts, and then quite a bit of fiddling back and forth on the computer.

'I always consider the changes suggested by the editors, and probably use about 70 per cent of their ideas. I look at the ideas and think: "Is it a good idea? Can it be used? Will the idea damage the flow of the story?" Sometimes an idea is good, but I've got to fiddle around with it to work it in.'

ROBERT CORMIER

'I never show anyone my work while I'm writing, and I only show my editor the finished manuscript. This doesn't mean that I won't rewrite that manuscript again. After I've finished I'm very open to suggestions on how to make it better. At the end of writing a novel, I've lost my perspective and can't stand off from the novel and see it. Editors can be very helpful in this. They aren't emotionally involved and can see the weaknesses.

'However, I'm very selective about the suggestions I use. I use those which I think are for the good of the book. I'm a mild-mannered person but when it comes to writing, I'm at the typewriter and I'm in command.'

CYNTHIA VOIGT

'My family and my editor read my manuscripts before I think that they're complete. However, they don't read them until each chapter is complete, and I take notice of what they say. My daughter Jessie read *Homecoming* chapter by chapter when she was eight. I don't ask my daughter to give me a report, but I watch whether she wants to keep reading the book.

'My editor tells me if they want to publish the book,

and usually asks me to cut the length. I listen to her suggestions, but I also know that people have blind spots and I try to juggle what she says with what I know about how she responds to a book.

'I use the responses from my family and my editor more to warn me that something isn't working, rather than to tell me what to do with it. I then go back and revise the manuscript further.

'Revision as I'm writing the story is what gives my characters strong personalities and identities. Those identities don't happen as a single creative thought. They've been worked on through revising over and over again. I use revision again, on completing the manuscript, to balance the portrayal of a character. One of the first things I ever do in a revision is worry about whether I've done a fair job on a character.'

LEE HARDING

'I can't tell if my writing is good. I can only tell if it might do. The writer is just so close to the finished work. I think it's important to be able to stand back and be your own editor, if possible. There's a very simple way to do this, and that is to write the sort of book that you'd like to read.

'Most writers are well read. They have to be. So it helps to look at your writing and say: "How would Robert Cormier have handled this scene?" Or: "How would Leon Garfield have done that?" It helps to measure yourself against writers you admire—to understand their technical skill, and compare it to your own.

'It's very important to look at your work as a piece of fiction, and see how it looks on the page. It's important to see where the dialogue works, or to see where the narrative is vague or unclear. The way that I do this is, when I've finished my draft, I put it away in a drawer for three months. I do something else and forget about it, and hopefully come back to it with a more detached eye.

'I never let anyone read my manuscripts while they're still in their draft form. It doesn't help to be overpraised by friends—or criticised, which can very easily discourage you. So writing can be a very lonely thing to do. The sort of writing that goes down deep and is revealing of myself is very private, and can't easily be shared during the struggle to write it down.

'When my book is ready to be read, the editor becomes very important. Think of all the balls the writer, like a juggler, is trying to keep up in the air and working. They've got one ball up in the air—that's the story. They've got another one which is characters. They've got another one which is dialogue. They've got another one which is pace, another one which is atmosphere, as well as spelling and syntax. Occasionally I fumble, and drop one of them, because I'm too close to what I've written. The advantage of revision is that I have a chance to go back and correct these things. But in the revision I become so familiar with what I've written that my eyes just glide over things. This is the advantage of having an editor or publisher's reader read the manuscript.'

MICHAEL DUGAN

'I don't show progressive drafts to anyone else. The first person to see my manuscripts is the publisher's editor. However, an exception is nonsense verse, because I'll sometimes read draft nonsense poems to a class group and make changes after getting their response.

'Editors, and the publisher's readers who advise them, play a most important role in the author's life. No writer can take a detached view of his or her own work. By the time a book is finished you're far too closely involved with it for this.

'The editor looks at the manuscript with a clear and

independent eye, and often notices inconsistencies or faults that the author has missed.

'Sometimes an editor's opinion may conflict with the author's opinion, and then it's up to one of them to convince the other that he or she is right, or for them to agree to a compromise. A good editor is someone with a lot of experience in making good books better, and any writer who didn't pay attention to their advice would be most unwise. I have often rewritten sections of books after discussions with my editors.'

ROBERT LEESON

'My editors comment on what I've written, and sometimes ask me to do some rewriting. Apart from my family, my editors are very often my first readers, and their point of view is important because so far you've only seen the book as you see it yourself. It's important to listen carefully to what the editors say. A good editor is the one who knows what the author is trying to say, and intends to help them say it successfully. Therefore, any suggestions that the editor can make which will make my book more successful are very welcome.

'If an editor is trying to change what I'm saying, then I think I've got to be very firm about what I believe in. When I wrote *It's My Life*, which is about a teenage girl, certain editors read it and altogether they sent me sixty-three different comments on the book. I accepted thirty-five of them and didn't accept the rest. This was because I trusted them, and the best work is done when you can discuss it carefully and sort out what's the best way of producing the kind of story you want.

'In my books, generally, because I've spent so long over working out the plot before writing, there are not very often changes of that kind to be made. But I think it's a very valuable way of going about things to have someone read the book carefully, intelligently and sympathetically, and point out where I'm not really succeeding in getting over what I want.

'Then, I think, it's important to be left to put it right myself.'

Historical Fiction

ROSEMARY SUTCLIFF

'I change what I'm writing if as I work there's something in myself which says: "Is this all right? Yes, it is. No, it isn't."

'I'd be rather surprised and annoyed if an editor asked me to change something in my story after I'd sent the finished manuscript. But I wouldn't be disagreeable about it. I'd try to do what the editor asked if it was possible, but I have dug my toes in and refused when it was unnatural to the character.'

Poetry

'I now know much more when a poem is good or bad than I did even five years ago. I know what's right, and what's almost right, and what's completely wrong.

'My editor has given me very good ideas about how to look at my own work, and I think I'm learning all the time. But, ultimately, I have to make all my own choices.'

Jack Prelutsky

EVE MERRIAM

'I've had all kinds of editors. I don't like the editor who just leaves it all to me as much as the editor who'll really work with me. Editors help me most by telling me when they don't understand what my poem is about. Sometimes a poem is too personal, in the sense that other people don't know what I'm talking about.

'I usually fight an editor who tells me what age group would enjoy my poems, because any age can go for poetry. So I don't like to take poems out when I'm told by the editor that they're for the wrong age group.

'When I do listen is if I'm not making the poem clear in what it says, or if the editors can see a "bump" in the line. This is embarrassing, because I pride myself on having a wonderful sense of rhyme and rhythm. But I can miss seeing a "bump". For example, Gilbert and Sullivan wrote the lines:

> "When you're lying awake with a dreadful headache and the bedclothes are all about you . . ."

If the line were to be

> "When you're lying very much awake with a headache . . ."

then that's a "bump", because there's too much in the first line. Someone else, like an editor, can sometimes see that much more clearly than I can.

'I now have some say, along with the editor, as to how my poems are actually going to be printed—how they're going to look on the page, what poem will go on what page and alongside what other poem, where it will be positioned on the page, and so on. This is important, but I didn't get that when I first began. I had to establish myself a great deal to be able to have that sort of say. Otherwise, it's all in the hands of the editor and the designer, and generally, you should go along with this.'

Non-Fiction

SEYMOUR SIMON

'After I think that I've finished the book I put it away for a few days, or a few weeks. Then I come back to it and I read it as if it's somebody else's work and I'm reading it for the first time. I become an editor and I see if there's any place that I think can be improved. If I feel that I've said what I wanted to say as well as I could, then I send it to my editor. Because I rewrite so much as I work, I rarely get a manuscript sent back because it's no good.

'My editor will suggest changes such as rearranging the sequence, or moving something from one place to another, because he thinks that it's clearer that way. But these aren't demands. We discuss them, and if I agree with some or all of the suggestions, I'll make the changes and send the manuscript back to him. Then the copy editor goes through it and pencils in changes which have to do with the sort of punctuation, or use of capitals or rules for writing numbers, which that particular publisher likes to use.

'Because some of my books are photo-essay books, where the photographs are actually collected and chosen by me, I have a lot of say about what illustrations are used. The design of the book, however, is done by a designer and the art director, so I don't have much say in that. The editor does usually ask me if I'm happy if they use a certain artist for other types of illustration, but I don't have any final say about it. I can discuss the illustrations with the artist and editor, and I do check the drawings for correct scientific content, but if I don't like them then I usually just have to put up with it.'

AFTER PUBLICATION

MAX DANN

'I'm usually never happy with how a book of mine looks or how it reads by the time it's been published, so I promptly forget about it. It's important to me what people think about it, but I don't really want to talk about it at all, I just want to get on with the next thing.

'The book has usually taken a year to publish since I've finished writing it, so I'm well and truly doing several other things and it isn't difficult to forget about that earlier book.

'I don't worry too much any more about what critics say about my books, though it's hard not to be affected. I'm learning to live with what they say.'

MICHAEL DUGAN

'Once a book has been published I like to have a nice clean copy to sit on my shelves. But, generally speaking, the process is over for me and I lose interest in the book (though not in its sales!). This is partly because, by the time of production, I'm heavily involved in writing another book.'

MICHAEL FOREMAN

'I almost never look at my books again, once they're in print. That's because while I'm actually writing and illustrating them, I'm on a high. Then when they're finished I feel nothing, because after a year I usually only like a bit of the book. Most of it is a total embarrassment to me, and I know that the book is going to be around for a long time. I feel that I'd really like to redo a lot of my earlier books.

'The only one that I've really thought about afterwards is *Land of Dreams*, because it turned out to be better than I thought it was. It was a long time coming, and while I think the illustrations could be better, I like its strange ideas.'

SIMON FRENCH

'Newspaper and magazine reviews always count, because they're really the only way many people get to find out about new childrens' books. Reaction from reviewers has often been favourable, but I've taught myself to live with the criticism that also invariably occurs—to regard it as a challenge of sorts. More vital to me is the feedback from children who happen upon my stories and feel motivated enough to write me letters conveying opinions and reactions to my books. The analogies they sometimes draw between what I've written about, and their own lives, can be often very touching.'

VICTOR KELLEHER

'At the end of a book, I usually feel that this isn't one of my best books. I'm so tired of it, I've been so close to it, that all I want to do is get away. And sometimes I'm right: it's not one of my best books. But I know that I've made it into as good a book as I can make it.

'My writing began out of a need to cope with certain things, and still is a little bit like that. Therefore, I don't really try to only write books that will sell, which is probably not very sensible.

'I don't mind what people say about my books, as long as what they say is intelligent.

ROBIN KLEIN

'I never get over the thrill of the published book. When I get my advance copy I don't do any work for the rest of the day. I sit down and read the book from cover to cover. And because there's usually such a long gap between when I wrote it and when it was published, it's almost like meeting the story for the first time.'

'I have to have a sense of my own worth as a writer, because even after a book has been published, there will be people who will criticise it, and people who won't like it when they read it. But that is all right, because the first person I write the story for is myself.'

Jane Yolen

WHY WRITERS WRITE

LLOYD· ALEXANDER

'I have a compulsion to write. I must do it. If I don't write, I can't live with myself. It hurts more not to write than it does to write. However painful the process may be, I'm dealing with some part of myself. It's something I do to stay alive, and I don't mean making my living.

'It will never make me famous, and it will never make me rich, but writing is how I stay alive and stay sane.'

ALLAN BAILLIE

'One reason I write is because I can write, and because there are a certain number of things I want to say. But more than that, I've learnt that I can create a character. Perhaps not in the first draft, or even the second, but when that character begins to take off, it's more exciting than winning the America's Cup.

'I also get a very big kick from realising that there are kids who read my stories, sometimes when they won't read anything else.'

'I write because reading meant so much to me when I was growing up, as it still does. I love reading, so naturally I like to write.'

Beverly Cleary

ROBERT CORMIER

'I think I'd explode if I didn't write. I'd be in a mental institution because where else would all these feelings go? I can't imagine not writing. It's like a little secret joy I carry around with me because it's something I can do. It gives my response to life a little extra dimension, because I observe something and I know I can capture it later.'

MAX DANN

'I think I know why I started to write. When I was at school I wasn't a great student. I was inept at most things. My grade 3 teacher got us to write a composition, and he read mine out to the class. He said that this was the way a composition should be written. For me, it was the only thing that I can remember that I was any good at in school. So I thought: "Well, maybe that's what I can do." Once I left school, I started to write and read as much as I could. I aimed to become a writer, even though I didn't know anything about it.

'But writing is very lonely. I sit in a room by myself for six or eight hours each day, and I don't really talk to anybody or see them. I need to write like this, because if there's anyone in the house, I can't write. If there's someone hammering something four houses away, I can't write. For me, writing requires absolute isolation. I sometimes feel that because I'm writing, I'm missing out on the world a bit.'

MICHAEL DUGAN

'I've always written, or at least as long as I can remember. Consequently, I now feel rather uncomfortable if I'm not involved in writing something. Once I have an idea for a book I want to follow it through, even if not immediately. My father was a journalist, and my mother has also written poems and articles, so it may be due to hereditary factors.

'Or, perhaps, it's some sort of virus!'

SIMON FRENCH

'It's something I've always enjoyed doing. I wanted to write even more when I got to high school and found that a lot of the books on the library shelves weren't about Australian children, and that the kids I was at school with weren't reading them.

'I began writing with these issues in mind, and the motivation further increased as the kids in my class began relating really well to what I was writing — not only because they saw their names in print on my typewritten foolscap pages, but also because the story I was piecing together was about what they were doing and thinking. It was their lives and their experiences of being twelve, thirteen, fourteen.

'I liked having my ideas challenged by books when I was at school. I also liked reading books that related to me and the way I was thinking. The books that still are important to me are encouraging in that they have ideas and situations which make me realise that other people go through the same sorts of things that I do.

'I have that in mind when I write, and my characters tend to be kids who are a little outside of the mainstream. I like presenting ideas that touch someone somewhere; that touch upon their lives and make them feel better about themselves, or about others.'

'I always liked reading, and so I wanted to write. I've done several things in my life. I've been a photographer and I've managed a bookshop. But I've always loved literature. I love words. If I could start again I'd like to direct movies. I'm a storyteller. I like to take the reader and, with my stories, raise questions — shake them, so that hopefully, when they've finished reading the book, they might look around them a bit more closely and see that the world is so much more rich and strange than they ever imagined.'

Lee Harding

VICTOR KELLEHER

'I started late, as a writer. I started, not intending to be a writer. I started because before I came to Australia I'd lived most of my life in Africa. I'd gone to New Zealand, and suddenly, for the first time in my life, I was overpoweringly filled with painful homesickness for my life in Africa. I couldn't cope with it. But I certainly knew that I wasn't going back to Africa. So to try and cope with my homesickness, I sat down and wrote about my memories, to get them out into the open. Then I began to re-pattern them to make sense of them, and they gradually became fictions and then short stories.

'Writing is very hard work and often makes me quite miserable. But writing also makes me happy through pattern-making with language, through knowing that I am making something, and through helping me deal with difficult feelings or events.

'One of the things that happens to you as a writer is that as you grow older, you discover that you can do all kinds of things that you thought you couldn't do — as long as you don't hide behind the settee for too long!'

STEVEN KELLOGG

'I love writing and drawing picture books. I love sharing the stories and characters. I feel compelled to do it. If I weren't doing it for my living, I'd be doing it in my spare time, and on the side, and on the sly! I consider myself very fortunate that my job is doing something that I absolutely love.'

ROBIN KLEIN

'It's like an addiction. I can't go for four days without writing. I become crabby and disagreeable. Because I came to writing fairly late, I feel that time is passing, and I haven't yet really written the book that I want to write.'

ROBERT LEESON

'I used to make up stories when I was about nine or ten, and we didn't have a school library. If I was satisfied enough with the story I'd tell close friends, and later on I got the idea of writing them down because my friends seemed to like them. So I think the reason why I write is because I want someone to read the stories. I want someone to hear what I've got to say. If I've got something I enjoy, my impulse is to share it with someone. My enjoyment is multiplied when I share it, and I suppose, really, that's the answer.'

'Writing for me is pain, torture and frustration—and surprise when it comes out well.'

Arnold Lobel

MADELEINE L'ENGLE

'I was a very solitary, only child, living in New York City during World War II. My father had been gassed in World War I and was very ill. This, plus all the horrible stories we were hearing about the war, made me very unhappy and confused. I found I could only find answers in stories, in putting characters into conflicts where they had to make creative or destructive decisions.

'I wrote my first story when I was five, and I've been writing stories, and reading stories, ever since.'

'I write poetry to live and to breathe. I couldn't live my life without writing poetry and reading poetry and having poetry in the world. It's just a way of understanding and holding on to the world as it goes spinning round the universe. It brings tidings of joy and comfort and love. It is my dearest companion.'

Eve Merriam

JACK PRELUTSKY

'Writing poetry is one of the three or four most enjoyable things I can think of doing. It comes out naturally. It's my gift, and I'd be foolish not to use that gift. Verse and rhythm and rhyme are just as much a part of me as breathing.

'I do it out of love. I do it for myself. I do it because I know children enjoy it. And I also do it for a living.'

'I'm in love with words. I've been a writer since I learnt how to read, and I've been a reader all my life. The idea of actually using words and creating something for myself has always excited me. Putting words together in a way which is unique to me is something I still think is one of the most thrilling things that one can do in one's life.'

Seymour Simon

ROSEMARY SUTCLIFF

'I write because I want to. I write because the stories are inside me and they want to come out. I don't always enjoy writing, because it's hard work. But if I don't write, I get this awful feeling of being all stuck up and turning into concrete inside. When I start writing and everything comes flowing out, I feel looser and more relaxed.

'Making the story and the people come to life has got to come from inside me. So I'm doing this funny thing of spinning real people out of my own interior, like a spider spinning silk. These things come from inside myself and it can be a most eerie sensation. It's very exciting.'

SUE TOWNSEND

'I'd go mad if I didn't write. It's my way of seeing and understanding my life. It helps me make sense of it.

Without writing, I think my brain would just spiral out. I need to do it.

'When I was a child I thought I was barmy because I had sentences forming in my head all the while. I wrote awful, terrible, pretentious things. It took me until I was about sixteen or seventeen to think that I could be a writer.

'It's nice to be able to say I'm a writer. I'm very proud of it. I think it's a wonderful thing to be.'

CYNTHIA VOIGT

'I write because I want to. I write for the reason that you do anything that you think you're good at: because I enjoy it. In a book I have my universe where I can try out things and see, "What would happen if . . .?"

'I write because I get a vision of a story that wants to be told. That vision is absolutely perfect—it has no flaws. And I want to make that story. I want to see it. That's the reason I write.'

JANE YOLEN

'I wanted to be a ballet-dancer for a while, and I learnt ballet for many years until I hit puberty and started growing wider instead of taller. Then I wanted to own a horse ranch, until I spent one summer mucking out the stables and discovered that I really didn't want to do that for the rest of my life. But I'd always written, for as long as I could remember, so I slowly began to realise that what I wanted to do was write fiction.

'I'm a compulsive writer. I get up in the morning and I have all these things inside me that want to come out. Sometimes I'm struck by a story that will never be told unless I tell it. And once I start telling it, I want to tell it in the very best way I can. It's never perfect when I write it down the first time, or the second time, or the fifth time. But it always gets better as I go over it and over it.

'So many story ideas keep coming in at me that it's a bit like turning on the radio and getting too many stations tuned in at the same time. They all mix together and I can't quite sort them out. When that happens, I have to make everything go blank to try and stop them. But when I've homed in on one station, and it's coming in clear and right through my fingertips and on to the page, then it's very exciting.'

ACKNOWLEDGEMENTS

The editor and publishers gratefully acknowledge the following companies for allowing us to reproduce copyright photographs:

Century Hutchinson London for the photograph of Michael Foreman.

Oxford University Press Australia for the photograph of Max Dann.

Penguin Books Australia Ltd for the photographs of Lee Harding and Victor Kelleher.

AUTHOR INDEX

TITLE INDEX